The Long Siege:Danzig,1813

The Long Siege:Danzig,1813

The Siege of Dantzic, in 1813
Louis Antoine François de Marchangy

Dantzig and Poland:The Background &
History of the Siege of Dantzig, 1813
(Extract)
Simon Askenazy

LEONAUR

The Long Siege:Danzig, 1813
The Siege of Dantzic, in 1813
By Louis Antoine François de Marchangy
Dantzig and Poland:The Background & History of the Siege of Dantzig, 1813
(Extract)
By Simon Askenazy

First published under the titles
The Siege of Dantzic, in 1813
and
Dantzig and Poland (Extract)

FIRST EDITION

Leonaur is an imprint
of Oakpast Ltd

ISBN: 978-1-78282-261-5 (hardcover)
ISBN: 978-1-78282-262-2 (softcover)

http://www.leonaur.com

Contents

The Siege of Dantzic, in 1813

Contents

Ferte cito ferrum, date tela, scandite muros
Hostis adest eja!

—Virg. .Eueid, L. IX,V, 37 & 38.

PLAN
DU SIÈGE
de
DANTZIG.

ILE DE NEHRUNG

Communication du Port

Heubude

F.t de Weichselmunde

Camp de
Neufahrwasser

ILE de HOLM

Pietule

lac de Saspe

RADE

Scholl-muhl

Breesen

Rothhof

Neu Scotland

Langenfü

Nord

Striessen

INONDATION

Redoute prussienne

Mottlau

Neuer Weg

Ohra

St. de Petersbourg
brise

St. Schidlitz

Chemin de Borschau

Stolzenberg

Schid

Zigankenberg

Kraus

Wonnenberg

Tempelburg

Pietschendorf

Wochau

Melle Toises

The Siege of Dantzic in 1813

France has been invaded, (1814), but not vanquished, nor is her military glory eclipsed, by those events which have preceded the return of the Bourbons. Even the coalesced powers, those who partitioned Poland, after having conquered it, entered on our territory with that respect, which those heroic deeds, that for twenty years have shed an illustrious splendour on the French Arms, demanded from them. Our trophies still remain unmoved, our standards are yet erect; nor should the confidence inspired by our physical strength be weakened, by those occurrences which have taken place.

Why then, instead of demonstrating those great and sublime truths, to which, it would be, perhaps, necessary to call the attention of the French People, at a moment when reverses may have humiliated, and sunk them in their own opinion, or at least have saddened and discouraged them, why have writers in pamphlets and newspapers devoted their pens to political subjects, touched upon in the most superficial manner? Rarely do we see that polemical writings, or even deliberative assemblies, produce happy results for the public weal, and in a government like ours, it would be perhaps better, according to an expression used by Marshal, the Prince de Ligne, that our confidence should be greater, and our laws less.

The plain unadorned recital of facts, which illustrate national honour, is undoubtedly far preferable to the systems, remonstrances, and discussions of pretended politicians, whose seeming zeal is stimulated by intrigue, necessity, or vanity. Our ancestors read very little, except those books which narrated the glorious feats and achievements, of a few illustrious characters. Their study was the lives of a Bertrand du Guesclin, of a La Hire, or of a Bayard, yet they possessed as much courage, loyalty and wisdom, as we do, and their happiness was greater.

Those reflections have induced me to give an exact detail of a siege, honourable to the French name; whatever may have been the government, under which the glorious deeds I am about to relate have been performed, they now form a part of the inheritance of the Bourbons, and the laurels which adorn the brows of our heroes, are now closely interwoven with the Lilies of the Crown.

The siege of Dantzic of which I shall give a faithful history, forms one of the most interesting episodes of the late war. If we had in the relation of this event only to consider, the bravery of our soldiers, or those military virtues, which shone with splendour in almost all the sieges our arms have sustained, a particular and circumstantial recital would be unnecessary; but a concurrence of unheard of circumstances, renders the siege of Dantzic, more remarkable than any event of the kind we read of. We cannot hear without emotion, of those French soldiers, who for an entire year, braved with resignation and intrepidity, the complicated horrors of hunger, cold, pestilence, and war, separated from their beloved country, by a distance of twelve hundred miles, and surrounded by numerous armies, and entire nations panting for their destruction.

The chief of the French Government has been generally blamed, for having left amidst remote ramparts, bounded by frozen waters, so many brave men, whose courage was unavailing to the operations that were to be pursued, such is the judgment formed of the determination to keep possession of Dantzic, from the sad termination which resulted; but the situation of Napoleon, imposed on him the duty of holding that important place, where he had vast magazines, one hundred and twenty thousand muskets, an immense depot of grain and clothing, and twelve millions, raised off the Duchy of Courland.

Those magazines and riches which could not be carried off, amidst the disorder and precipitate retreat, which in an unforeseen manner terminated the campaign of Moscow, would alone have been sufficient to justify the resistance made at Dantzic, had not a motive still more noble, rendered its preservation an imperious duty. The thirtieth division of infantry, and fifteen hundred dragoons cantoned in Mecklenburg, had received peremptory orders to march towards Keoningsberg, to support the grand army, which from the rigour of a dreadful season, and the efforts of an enemy, whose confidence and boldness were encouraged by our misfortunes, fell back on every side.

This division was fifteen thousand men strong, if that character could be given to youthful conscripts, of which it was almost entirely composed. The fatigue of forced marches had wasted away the strength of those feeble soldiers, when on their arrival at Labiau, they were witnesses of the tumultuous retreat of the wreck of the grand army. Rallied by the corps of Marshal the Duke of Tarentum (Macdonald,) they made good a retreat the miseries of which they could not much longer have supported; had they been obliged to sustain a few marches more, those harassed soldiers, would have fallen into the hands of the enemy, or must have remained on the Prussian roads, had not the gates of Dantzic been opened to offer them a refuge. A vast number of other troops, and particularly a train of artillery, consisting of sixty pieces of cannon arrived about the same time in the city. On taking an account of the force of the garrison, the numbers amounted to thirty-three thousand men, but by a most singular diversity, and which must evince the disorderly retreat from Moscow, those thirty-three thousand men belonged to a number of different nations.

Count Rapp was the Governor of Dantzic, nor was it possible to confide a post of equal peril and difficulty, to one better calculated to fulfil its arduous duties; he was equally fitted to animate the energy of his troops, by the example of his own brilliant valour, or to give spirit to the hopes of those who sought for honours or advancement, by the very great influence and weight, which the attachment of this highly distinguished officer, to the Emperor Napoleon, had merited from him. The governor was nobly supported by generals of the first merit. M. Campredon, general of division, commanded the engineers, the direction of which corps was entrusted to M. Richmont, colonel of that corps, an officer brave and indefatigable, animated by the most romantic honour, and recalling to memory those chivalric virtues attached to his name. General Lepin, so eminently distinguished by those talents which placed him in the first rank, of superior officers, commanded the artillery. The divisions of infantry were under the orders of the Generals Heudelet and Grandjean, both equally fitted to advise in council, or direct in battle; under the command of the latter, was a Corps of Bavarians and Poles, amongst whom shone particularly conspicuous the brave and amiable Prince Michael Radzivill.

General Detres *aide de camp* to the King of Naples, was at the head of the division of Neapolitans, General Cavaignac commanded two thousand horse; the marine was under the direction of Rear Admiral Dumanoir; Monsieur de Herecourt filled the duties of Major General, Chief of the Staff; the long residence of this officer in Dantzic, joined to his personal merit, made him valuable in a double capacity. M. Bartoneuf directed the management of civil affairs, with equal zeal, and disinterestedness.

Dantzic, situated at the Mouth of the Vistula, and washed on one side by that river, is one of the most considerable cities of the continent, by its size, commerce, riches, and strength. To the north it is covered by vast inundations, which at that side render it inaccessible, on the South it is defended by formidable redoubts, on its walls were mounted six hundred pieces of cannon.

However, the immense works ordered by the Emperor Napoleon, had not yet been finished, and the system of defence was as yet imperfect; but what particularly alarmed the garrison, was the dreadful coldness of the weather which had frozen the immense waters, by which one side of the city was protected, in such a manner, that those mounds and marshes formed by nature to serve as a kind of humid rampart for its defence, became transformed into solid plains, which might easily afford to the besiegers access to the place. In order to oppose anew to the enemy, a barrier of waters, the officers of engineers determined on breaking theice. This was an incessant task, painful and destructive to a crowd of soldiers, who fatigued by the consequences of the last campaign, could ill support this laborious toil and drudgery—disturbed by the enemy, benumbed by the frost, and beat down by the northern blasts, every moment at the hazard of disappearing amidst the waves, they went from one sheet of ice to another, endeavouring to break during the day, the brittle vault which the winter's night still closed around them.

Amongst the soldiers employed in this manner, were eight hundred Spaniards, in the service of France, who far distant from the lovely, fertile plains of Castile and Andalusia, shared a warlike banishment in those northern regions—but why recall the remembrance of the first miseries we endured, when almost at the very beginning of the siege, a dreadful scourge appeared, and demands the melancholy tribute of those sorrows and tears, which a feeling mind cannot refuse to the unfortunate victims it destroyed, when on the retreat of the French Army from Moscow, its sad reverses were exposed through Russia, Poland and Prussia, a great part of the sick which accompanied it, was left behind in the different villages, through which it forced itself a passage. Dantzic had received already ten thousand of these victims, but by an oversight of which, almost all strong places afford 'a melancholy example, it had neither hospitals, beds, or supplies of any kind prepared; there were not even provisions for the sick, or necessary medicines.

The requisitions demanded from the inhabitants, could not promptly enough relieve their absolute, immediate, and necessary wants, the sick without shelter, or medical attendance, implored in vain from the compassion of the inhabitants, a little straw on which they might rest their heads, inflamed by the heat of a burning fever. Those unfortunate men, conquerors of Smolensko and Moscow, expired daily from the moment they had reached Dantzic. Warm quarters, wholesome diet, and linen to dress their wounds, would have saved their lives, but deprived of those necessaries, essential to their existence, they perished; and the pestilential exhalations which issued from this mass of putrid bodies, collected within a small circle, spread on every side an epidemic disease, which indiscriminately seized on both citizens and soldiers.

Attacked by a dreadful and incurable disorder, disseminated by the contagious air of the city, the soldiers almost regretted their escape from the devouring flames of Moscow, the watery gulphs of the Beresina, or the dreary snows of Lithuania. Through the streets of Dantzic, those dying victims, covered with rags, were seen wandering along accosting the passengers with wild laughter or vacant folly, and all those concomitant signs of distraction, and delirium, which attended this disorder. Three hundred persons daily died of it. The Generals, Franceschy and Gault, were amongst its first victims. Crowds of individuals of every sex, age, and rank, followed without interruption; and every quarter of this great city, became the scene of sorrow, and of mourning.

The funeral procession of the senator, was only interrupted by the military obsequies paid to the French officer, and the same grave received forever within its silent bosom, the Pole, the Batavian, the Tuscan, Saxon, Spaniard, Westphalian, Bavarian, Neapolitan, and Frenchman; during the last moment of their existence, those different foreigners, burning with the love of their native soil, in vain, wildly invoked their beloved families and friends and called out for their country, which, alas! they were destined never more to behold.

General Rapp quickly knew, that the enemy was acquainted with the destruction, which the epidemic disease caused in the place they had invested. In order to deprive him of information of the dreadful losses he sustained, all funeral ceremonies, attendants, and parade, were forbidden.

From that time, neither the mournful sound of the muffled drum, nor the salute fired over the grave of the hero were any longer heard at his interment. One only saw the funeral procession of the citizens, followed by a melancholy few, composed of relations and friends, dressed in mourning. The grave diggers were ordered to carry off privately the bodies of the dead, and a widow, a sister, or a child, in spite of their emotions, obliged to stifle their sorrows; formed the only escort that accompanied the beloved object they had lost to the grave. During these clandestine burials, death brought its victims to the terrible level of equality, and in those frightful moments, there was nothing to soothe or disguise the horrors of dissolution. The plague carried off twelve thousand of the inhabitants, and twenty-one thousand soldiers. Ten thousand men, able to carry arms, scarcely remained.

At a moment when this small number, appeared insufficient to guard the interior fortified works of Dantzic, the governor undertook to defend, not only the body of the place, but even the immense suburbs, which, towards the south, extend beyond the ramparts, to a considerable distance. The critical situation of the French, rendered this determination rash; perhaps even according to military science, and the unfeeling rules which regulate an obstinate defence, General Rapp might be deemed culpable in not having concentrated his operations within the interior of the place, and in having weakened his means of resistance, by occupying those large suburbs, open on every side to attack, and in which it was impossible to hold out, unless by extraordinary vigilance and unheard of efforts; but French bravery was flattered by the field that was opened to its exploits from this resolve; and humanity will proudly record, as the noblest trait in his character,.

The unceasing efforts of the governor, to preserve, uninjured, the suburbs which, from, their grandeur, wealth, and population, formed the most considerable part of Dantzic. Had General Rapp determined not to defend them, he would have been obliged according to the barbarous policy of war, to burn and destroy them, in order to render them useless to the enemy. In yielding up to humanity this horrible right, Count Rapp conciliated the minds of all the inhabitants of Dantzic, who from that moment became devoted to him through a sentiment of gratitude, and no longer felt repugnance in relieving and ameliorating the different wants of the garrison.

The Russians manoeuvred in the environs of the place, blockading the different passages from it, and it became highly important to the besieged to get information of their numbers, designs, and positions; but however great the temptations held out to the avarice of the inhabitants of the country, who alone were calculated for the dangerous duty of obtaining intelligence; during the first part of the siege, it was almost impossible, to procure any one to undertake the office. If the kind conduct of the French towards the inhabitants of Dantzic had triumphed over their natural aversion, it could not diminish their wishes to see that city occupied by the Russians, in order that their harbour, which, by its trade and industry, constituted their prosperity, might once more be thrown open to the commerce of England.

This deficiency of spies devoted to the garrison left the governor in a state of uncertainty and hesitation which threw a damp on every kind of enterprise. Dreading a *coup de main* or stratagem, which it was almost impossible to foresee or prevent, it became necessary to multiply the sentinels, the patrols, and videttes, even often to call the garrison to arms; thus kept in a continual state of watchfulness, the soldiers wearied by the fatigues of the day, were torn from the repose they required at night, their strength became weakened, but nothing could diminish their ardour and their zeal.

When General Rapp was so fortunate as to gain over some to act as spies, their intelligence was almost always defective, from the unexpected and extraordinary movements which took place during the siege, and the variety of changes and alterations in the Russian armies; for at this particular period, their troops eagerly pressed upon the rear of our grand army, retreating in disorder, and only appearing in the environs of Dantzic, then pursued their route. At times they reconnoitred the place for a number of days—then other corps succeeded to the blockade, who still yielded their places to new battalions. Thus Dantzic beheld almost all the corps of the Russian Army, yet in the interior of the place, they could form no judgment of the forces which surrounded it.

All that could be learned positively was, that General Platoff was one of the first who arrived there, at the head of eighty thousand men, composed partly of Cossacks and Basquirs. These communications did not alarm the garrison; it heard with delight the orders it received to make partial sorties to the distance of two or three leagues from the city. These daily excursions had in view the threefold objects of exercising the soldiers, of pushing forward the reconnoitring parties towards the advanced posts of the enemy, and of procuring in the neighbouring fields, cattle and forage, of which the place was in want.

Those dangerous expeditions, unexpected rencontres and repeated skirmishes, gave opportunity to numbers of our military enthusiasts to display their valour and determined bravery. A variety of such affairs took place from the 10th of January, 1813, to the 5th of March ensuing, on which day a general engagement took place. Meanwhile disease daily continued to prey upon its victims; and, great as the precautions were which the governor observed, the Russians became acquainted with the weakness of the garrison, now reduced to one-third of its original strength. They supposed, that an assault boldly made on every side, and with overwhelming forces, would be sufficient to carry a place laid desolate by a permanent disease.

On the 5th of March, they attacked with fury the suburbs, the most important of which were Stoltzenburgh, Ohra, and Schidlitz. which situations had been made the depots of the Baltic trade; and also Langfuhr, a place remarkable for the beauty of its plantations, gardens, and the enchanting summer retreats with which it abounded. On the approach of the Russians, the French troops, to whom the defence of those suburbs was committed, assembled instantaneously; the enemy pushed forward with his principal force from the entrances which are in the rear of Langfuhr, and wished to seize on the fortified houses which terminate the avenue leading to this suburb. On every side a brave resistance disconcerted his projects.

However, after the most heroic efforts of both parties, the enemy became masters of the village of Stries, which gave them possession of the first buildings in Langfuhr. The suburbs of Stoltzenburgh and Schidlitz were attacked and defended with equal ardour. Thrice was this last quarter taken possession of by the enemy, and as often retaken by the thirtieth division, those very soldiers whose youth and debility have already been taken notice of, as rendering them unequal to the fatigues of war. Yet did national honour, and that emulative spirit, so quickly transfused into the hearts of Frenchmen, transform them into heroes. They almost seemed to increase in size and strengthen presence of the enemy; and, worthy of emulating the most intrepid veterans, they astonished, by their conduct, the Chief of Battalion Clement, who commanded with immoveable calmness this post, so violently assailed.

All the southern side of the place resounded with the noise of artillery, the clashing of arms, the shouts of the combatants, and the groans of a crowd of citizens and distracted females, whose firesides had become the scenes of a dreadful carnage—a number of posts had fallen into the power of the Russians, who had even penetrated into a part of the suburbs of Ohra, in spite of the excellent dispositions made by General Devilliers, who was wounded early in the action, and of the Chief of Battalion Bourant, who both arrested, with their troops, the rapid progress of an impetuous enemy. The Russians still continued to pour in their second columns when Count Rapp, informed of this general attack, ordered the troops in the interior to sally out; eagerly impatient, they burst open the gates of Dantzic, and flew with enthusiastic rapidity towards the suburbs: on sight of these reinforcements, whose decisive manoeuvres were directed by the governor, and executed by the General D'Heudelet and Grandjean, the enemy retired, astonished at the resistance made by men they had already deemed conquered by disease, and amazed to find those soldiers they supposed almost dying, still able to hurl defiance back upon their enemies.

General Grandjean had two horses wounded under him; the Sixth Neapolitan Regiment performed wonders on the plain it was charged to defend; Lieutenant General Detres had two horses killed, and nearly every officer of his staff wounded; Colonel Degonnara received several balls in his clothes. The Russians fell back with loss, and yielded, but in good order, the ground they had momentarily occupied, whilst they made along the whole of their line a retrograde movement; some thousands of them remained in the houses at Ohra and Langfuhr supposing their companions masters of the city, they only thought of enjoying in security the advantages of victory, and drinking, at their leisure, the excellent liqueurs which they found in abundance in the houses of the citizens.

The French generals, Bachelu and Breissand, made at the same moment a movement to surprise them; the first turned to the left, and rushing, at the head of the Poles, into the suburb of Ohra, disturbed by an attack entirely unexpected, the drunken carousals of the Russian soldiers, who, flying to their arms imagined, that in their numbers their imprudence would find impunity; but in a moment four hundred of them were pierced with the bayonet, and an equal number made prisoners. On his side, General Breissand, after having turned to the right, fell suddenly on the suburb of Langfuhr, where the enemy, astonished at seeing him, defended himself for a while, and was then put to the rout with immense loss.

The enemy, broken on all sides, evacuated the suburbs, and the garrison rushing in pursuit into the open country, pushed him back on the neighbouring heights; but night coming on, the fury of the battle lessened by degrees, the cannonade ceased, the victorious garrison returned to the city, and quickly the tumult of this honourable day was succeeded by a still silence, only interrupted at intervals by the challenge of the sentinels and videttes. This affair, in which the Russians lost two thousand men, and one piece of artillery, cost but a small number to the besieged, and was productive of the most important consequences. The Russians who had been made to feel the strength and prowess of those troops, who had been represented to them, by false reports, as weak and dispirited, became hereafter more circumspect in their attacks; and, except, with great precaution, hesitated to harass our advanced posts: they were made sensible, that a place so bravely defended could only fall by the efforts of a regular siege, in which patience would be more necessary than rashness.

From this period they kept back to a respectful distance, contenting themselves with occupying the entrances and roads leading to the place. Meantime, the return of the spring spread around the mild and genial influence of that lovely season; the weather, less severe, became softened by the rays of a vivifying sun; the north wind blew less violent; the snows began to dissolve; the waters, which washed a part of the walls, freed from their icy fetters, resumed their fluidity, and restored to the fortification a natural defence, which greatly diminished the labours, the watching, and fatigues of the besieged.

The effects of the return of spring, which seems to electrify nature, and to reanimate all beings relieved Dantzic from the alarm and terror in which it had been plunged by disease; the air became freed from contagious particles and putrid effluvia, and every day the epidemic distemper made less havoc. The situation of the hospitals ceased to be alarming; the soldiers who were in them became convalescent; and, after the horrors of a dreadful malady, and the rigorous frosts of a deadly winter, they tasted with transports the delight of returning health, and the sight of a vernal sun. As to those soldiers who had escaped sickness, the increase of their strength was not necessary to the support of an exhausted frame, and this fullness of health and life gave the most unbounded enjoyment to their imagination; brilliant hopes, fraught with dreams of glory and of happiness, began, to animate with their delusive prospects, the bosoms of those heroes, who, far distant from their country, had no means of safety left, but in their courage, and in their arms.

Recollecting the glorious days of Austerlitz, Jena, and Ratisbon, they believed that the Emperor Napoleon, who so often led them with rapidity from the North to the South, would quickly return on the wings of victory, to conduct them once more to the banks of the Vistula and the Niemen. In this expectation, they applauded themselves for having preserved, by their resistance, those immense and precious magazines, in which consisted the supplies for a war, which, according to their imaginations, they would yet carry into the heart of Russia. Whilst those ambitious and flattering hopes were indulged by the army, they were far from imagining the disastrous state to which their emperor had been reduced by the fortune of war. They could not suppose that he whom they beheld in idea appear once more victorious before their ramparts, should have been forced to quit the wrecks of his army, whilst the Russians entered into Berlin, and advanced even to Magdeburg.

They knew not that all Prussia had taken up arms against France, with an enthusiasm and fury which announced their determination to conquer or die; and that already she had assembled an army of two hundred thousand combatants. They were ignorant of the hostile intentions evinced by many of the allies of Napoleon, that Austria was preparing to march against him, and that Sweden had joined to the forces of the Coalition a large body of warlike troops, commanded by a Frenchman, the Prince Royal of Sweden. This news was calculated too well to disturb the garrison, to allow the besiegers to neglect giving them information of it. Every night the Cossacks, with equal boldness and rapidity, came up to our videttes, and fastened a lance near them, to which was affixed proclamations and journals, calculated to dissipate the error of the besieged, and to inform them of the wonderful military and political events which had taken place in Europe.

The governor became informed of the receipt of this intelligence; and, notwithstanding the distrust, doubt and suspicion, with which such information must be entertained, he felt that their accounts might have some foundation; for the scene of the retreat from Moscow returning then to his memory, allowed but little encouragement to incredulity, and his fears were constantly confirmed by the most circumstantial reports. The enemy often fired discharges of artillery, to announce pretended victories; all, however, were not fictitious; and the noise of cannon, accompanied by shouts of joy, proclaimed in their camp, the capture of Spandau and Thorn, the entrance into Dresden, and the occupation of almost all Saxony.

The besieged were not, however, discouraged, but they could not shut their eyes to the dangers they had to encounter; they were well aware that if Napoleon should be even successful in the approaching campaign, his march, opposed by innumerable obstacles, could not speedily conduct him to their deliverance. In the meanwhile, the place was defended by only a small number of men, divided amongst a variety of forts, entrenchments, and suburbs; it was deficient in every supply except grain; nor could provisions or forage, of which the horses were in great want, be procured, except at the point of the sword, from the surrounding country, exhausted by frequent incursions, and unable to afford farther supplies. Besides, the garrison had not the reviving reflection of knowing it was in the neighbourhood of a friendly nation.

The affrighted imagination was left to dwell on an immensity of dangers, in beholding the occupation of Poland by the Russians, and the declaration of war by Prussia. Separated by insurmountable barriers from France, the defenders of Dantzic seemed to have no alternative left them, but slavery or death. But what cannot a mighty strength of soul, united to a feeling of national honour, effect! The courage of the besieged redoubled in proportion to their danger, and all thoughts vanished from their hearts, except the glory of a heroic resistance. In order to give greater energy to the means of defence, the Generals Campredon and Lepin caused new works to be thrown up in the place; and different committees were formed, over which the superior officers presided, to act in concert with the government, in procuring provisions, regulating the finances, hospitals, and other important matters.

Those committees, arising from the difficulties of our situation, were the forerunners of vigorous measures, the execution of which became ruinous to numbers of the inhabitants of Dantzic, who were deprived, by numerous and indispensable requisitions, of whatever, might be useful to the garrison. By those means, beds, linen, wood, all kinds of provisions, and even two millions, were procured. The misery, which was overwhelming the garrison, was thrown on the population. Necessity and force, those two inflexible laws, bowed down, under their iron yoke, the wretched inhabitants of this Hanseatic town, which had been lately so flourishing and prosperous.

Meantime, the governor, disappointed in not having intelligence except through the medium of the enemy, which might be forged, or at least greatly exaggerated, resolved to procure more authentic information, by questioning the *burgomasters* of the neighbouring villages, and by directing the seizure of any journals, diaries, or official papers they might possess. To accomplish this purpose, it was necessary to undertake an expedition, particularly directed against the large village of Saint Albrecht, which was ordered to take place on the 24th of March, at the first dawn of the morning. The River Radaune, which in its course had turned a number of mills at Dantzic, until its current was turned off by the Russians, winds along the village.

The command of this sortie was confided to Count D'Heudelet. On the firing of the morning gun, all the disposable troops of the garrison assembled at the Petershagen Gate, which leads directly to the suburbs of Ohra. Whilst a part of the troops made false attacks on different points, the remainder manoeuvred with rapidity upon a plain, in the woods which lie before Ohra. Our soldiers in a moment were engaged on this side; the cavalry pushed forward; and, in a charge, in which Colonel Tasin highly distinguished himself, carried off two hundred men. At the same time, General Bacheli an officer of the greatest enterprise, and particularly fortunate in conducting sorties or unexpected attacks, led on the Polish infantry against a Russian corps, which he forced instantly to fly, by the fire of his artillery.

The banks of the river were covered with dead bodies, amongst which were numbers of a Russian corps of soldiers, who, in order to impress more terror on their adversaries had a Death's head affixed to the front of their caps, and had declared they would never give quarter, or make any prisoners; but their frightful appearance could not intimidate our soldiers, or hinder them from rushing on them with fury. A gunner of the name of Kraft, attacked by two Russians, killed one, and took the other; and a young Polish drummer fought a Russian grenadier, and made him prisoner, after a severe conflict. The Bavarian Major Seifferlitz, seeing a number of the enemy save themselves in the water, rushed in after them, and, followed by a few of his troop, pursued, and put them to the sword.

The enemy abandoned the village of Saint Albrecht, from whence our troops returned into the city, bringing with them some prisoners, provisions, and forage. They also were enabled, by this sortie, to acquaint the governor with the circumstantial accounts of the magistrates and country people, who all uniformly agreed in relating the progress of the enemy on the Saxon territory. The most useful effects resulted from the expedition to Saint Albrecht: as from it the governor ascertained, that the Russians were not in any great force, and that although their numbers were far superior to ours, yet he could attack them with impunity.

On the 18th day of April, being the hundredth day of the blockade, and Easter Sunday, the governor, in a moment of enterprising confidence, ordered the troops to parade beyond our advanced posts; several thousand men, infantry and cavalry, assembled at the distance of a league and a quarter from the city, in the beautiful plain shaded by the forest of Oliva. Our troops, with inconceivable boldness, slowly defiled amidst the flourishing of trumpets, at only fifteen *pares* from the enemy's lines, who remained motionless with astonishment.

The governor now thought a favourable opportunity had occurred, to permit an incursion into the surrounding country, in order to carry off cattle and forage in sufficient quantity to enable him to await the maturity of the harvest, which the surrounding fields gave promise of. To the east of Dantzic lies an extensive and fertile tract of country, called the Noehrung, one side of which is bounded by the Baltic, whose waves throw up on its banks an odoriferous amber; on two other sides it is enclosed by the Vistula, and forms a peninsula, ornamented with orchards, lakes, large plains, forests of fir, and full of small farms and fields, covered with numerous herds of cattle.

The inhabitants of this district are laborious and peaceful; however, it was into their possessions that the besieged resolved to make an irruption, in order to provision the place, the wants of which were every day growing more pressing. The 27th of April, troops marched out of the city, under the command of General Bachelu, to the number of fifteen hundred infantry, and two hundred cavalry. Our soldiers in a short time came up with the Russians, who guarded the roads towards the country; they rushed upon their first post. Colonel Reden, known in all the different armies, by thirty years of honourable service, was struck by four balls; the Commissary of War, M. Belissall, a brave soldier, fell wounded by his side; Colonels Baron Farine, Kiener, Nauman, Desseur and Kaminski, merited, by their conduct and bravery, the highest praises.

We made four hundred prisoners; the remainder was dispersed; and General Bachelu, after having forced this barrier, advanced into the country to the distance of eight leagues from Dantzic, and remained four entire days out of that city. We must contemplate with admiration, the *sang-froid* and contempt of danger displayed by this small number of men, who for such a length of time, and so far from their ramparts, dared to remain in a country covered with numerous battalions of the enemy, and full of inhabitants, whom the Tocsin could suddenly assemble against them. But so great are the excesses authorised by war, that the admiration we at first grant to the dauntless courage of the soldier, is quickly dissipated in reflecting on its dreadful consequences. For what was the course these men were obliged to take to supply a garrison, sinking under its privations and its wants? They rushed into the granaries and fields of the laborious peasant, to carry off his grain and flocks.

At the unexpected appearance of those troops, who had hazarded their safety, at such a distance from their fortifications, fear and desolation spread amongst those hamlets, so lately the abodes of peace; the soldiers eagerly poured in amidst those rural habitations, and seized on all the corn, cattle, and forage they could discover; whilst some collected the plunder, others conducted in haste the booty they had obtained, to the neighbouring banks of the Vistula, where the boats lay moored, which Rear Admiral Dumanoir had given orders to be ready to receive, and transport all that could be obtained to the walls of Dantzic.

The soldiers seized on the peasants, and forced them to assist in driving the numerous herds of cattle, which were increased in every village they passed through; and the labourer, with sighs, was obliged to yield up the heifer, whose milk gave nutriment to his children, and the oxen, the companions of his toils, to the wants of the garrison. However, to assuage the misery of these country people, and to soften the severity of the sacrifices they were compelled to make, the governor ordered, that bills, payable after the siege, on the French Treasury, should be delivered with the utmost expedition.

On the thirtieth of April the French troops returned to Dantzic, with eight hundred head of cattle, and forage for two months; the besieged received with shouts of joy those provisions, which enabled them to await with security the proper moment for gathering in the harvest. The environs of Dantzic, which, until now, the governor had been enabled, by means of videttes, field-works, piquets, advanced posts, and sharpshooters, to prevent the Russians from approaching, became clothed with a rich and abundant vegetation; and every day, a reviving dew, adding fresh verdure to the fields, gave vigour to the productions of the earth. The ground, which the besieged had as yet been enabled to preserve round the place, was the constant object of their vigilance and their cares: they reckoned on these future harvests as the means of prolonging their defence; and day and night they watched, with arms in their hands, the growing herbage, and green corn around them, with the same anxiety they would have guarded the treasures of Indostan.

The Russians, who wished to accelerate the surrender of Dantzic, by making famine an auxiliary to their designs, felt how important it was to deprive the garrison of those resources which nature was preparing for its support, and, in consequence, they resolved on making incessant attacks, in order to seize from the defenders of the place the possession of those fertile fields they held, and to shut them closely up within the walls of the city. The execution of this project appeared less difficult to the enemy, as he had received considerable reinforcements, and the command of the place had been entrusted to the Prince of Wurtemberg, uncle to the Emperor Alexander. The presence of this august personage before the walls of Dantzic, gave an assurance that the environs were soon to become the theatre of the most important operations. Immediately the tents and barracks of the enemy were extended on every side, and numerous detachments began to harass our videttes and advanced posts.

Every moment, night and day, it became necessary to fly to arms, in order to repulse those continual attacks. Often our soldiers, too weak to resist superior forces, found themselves obliged to give way, until the troops in the interior of the place hastened to their succour. A state of such continued alarm, marches and fighting, which allowed no repose to the French, redoubled their fatigues, and wasted away their diminished numbers. A thousand times were those growing harvests, they had as yet secured, bedewed with the blood and sweat of those heroes. They formed of their artillery, their bayonets, swords, and even of their very bodies, the enclosure of this land of promise, which, could it have had the power of bearing testimony to so many prodigies of valour, proud of such labourers, spontaneous laurels would have started up to cover its bosom, Count Rapp perceived that those incessant struggles, if not interrupted, would insensibly waste his troops, and that, in order to relieve himself from the wearying assaults of the besiegers, it became imperious on him to try a general engagement.

On the ninth of June, the governor ordered a general sortie of the entire garrison: the command of the right was given to General Grandjean; the left was entrusted to General Heudelet; General Heusson, at the head of six hundred picked men, and six pieces of cannon, passed the wood of Ohra, and, protected by the defence it formed, drew up his troops in advance; on his left was a hollow way, beyond which Major Schneider, with one hundred and fifty men, observed the road to Dirchau, a little more to the southward, and near the valley which extends from the side of Schonfield, General Cavaignac was placed with his cavalry, and some light artillery. General Breissand, with a number of battalions, had taken up a position near the suburbs of Stoltzenburgh, not far from which in the centre, in the valley of Schidlitz, General Devilliers was posted with the troops of the Confederation of the Rhine; lower down from Schidlitz to Langfuhr, General Grandjean, with his corps, kept the left of the enemy in observation; a strong force composed of Neapolitans, Bavarians and artillery, formed the reserve.

The ramparts of the city were covered with inhabitants, anxious to be spectators of the combat. As soon as the Russians saw our troops advance, they fired the alarm guns, lighted their signals, and united their forces. General Husson was the first who attacked the enemy, and merited, by the valour he displayed in this affair, the highest encomiums. Our artillery commenced its fire, the cannon of the enemy replied to it, and the engagement became serious on several points. The Russians, drawn up to the southward of the place, displayed their strength, and allowed us through the midst of clouds of smoke, to calculate their imposing numbers.

Four thousand of their infantry were stationed to the right of the village of Wonneburg, three thousand men were in front of General Husson, and two thousand had taken a position at the strong village of Pietzkendorf; the Russians, had besides those troops, fifteen pieces of cannon, and fifteen hundred cavalry—their united force was three times more numerous than the garrison; however, the French had a much more powerful artillery than the enemy, and, finding their superiority in that respect, they used it with such effect, that they dispersed with their cannon all the masses of infantry which were brought against them; some thousands of Cossacks began then to scatter themselves round our positions, and to disturb our sharpshooters; onetime they would unite to make a charge, they then in a moment dispersed, and, by the extreme rapidity of their movements, shewed themselves on every side, yet were not any where accessible to attack.

Although the French appeared too few in numbers to continue to support themselves against the enemy, they endeavoured to seize the opportunity afforded by this sortie, to gather forage and cut the corn, although, as yet, green in the fields they fought in; and during the time the greater part of the army was engaged on an advanced line, the remainder collected the plunder, loaded the wagons, and drove them into the city. Whilst the tremendous fire of thirty-five pieces of artillery from the troops commanded by General D'Heudelet, forced the army to give way, and retire in disorder behind the heights of Borgfeld and Miggau, the Russians, by a rapid movement, poured in with new battalions upon General Grandjean; both sides evinced the greatest bravery, attended with various success; the carnage was dreadful, and night alone terminated a battle in which the besieged had a great number wounded.

They did not lose so many killed as the enemy, whose loss in this affair could not be less than fifteen hundred men. But at the very time the besieged were fighting with such fury, a truce, in which they were comprehended, had been concluded between the Emperor Napoleon and the coalesced Powers. That great captain had fought, in the fields of Lutzen and Bautzen, two eventful battles, where each party claimed the honour, but which the French had reason to estimate as important victories. The political preponderancy, and military weight, which these events seemed to bestow on the chief of the French Government; the mediation of Austria, which, previous to an open declaration against Napoleon, wished, in appearance, to acquit herself of what she owed to the alliance she had contracted with him, by making some plausible efforts to procure peace; and indeed the necessity which all the Belligerent Powers had for a suspension of arms, induced the different parties to agree to an armistice.

All Germany rejoiced at this repose, which they considered as the forerunner of a general reconciliation; and Dresden, surrounded by peaceful camps, had become the scene of festivity and pleasure. Dantzic was as yet uninformed of these happy tidings; an officer dispatched from the grand army, charged with the intelligence, used the utmost expedition, in the hope of stopping the effusion of blood. Each step of this joyful messenger might save the life of a brave man: but in vain was his speed; he could not arrive until three hours after the battle of the 9th of June, when the environs of Dantzic were stained with the recent slaughter; the blood that had flown was yet smoking, and the bodies of the slain were scattered unburied on the fields.

The French officer, Captain Planat, shewed his dispatches at the headquarters of the enemy, and was permitted to enter the city; the governor received him, and immediately all the garrison and inhabitants of Dantzic, were informed of the armistice, and the events which had preceded it. After having remained such a length of time in a state of painful uncertainty, unacquainted with the fate of their fellow-soldiers, and the state of France, with what rapture did the besieged receive those consoling accounts! Transported with joy, they were all anxious to speak to each other, to communicate their thoughts, their sentiments, and their hopes; they accosted one another with smiles of delight beaming on their countenances. A siege of so many months—battles—privations—watching—sickness—sufferings and sorrows, were all forgotten. The officer was overwhelmed with questions; they interrogated eagerly all those with whom he had discoursed; they wished to know by what miracle the French, after the disasters of 1812, had all at once been enabled to repair such losses, and dispute the palm of victory with all the powers leagued against them.

Some sighed at the recital of battle, where they had not fought and conquered with their brothers in arms; others felt a pride in having preserved a city, which the successes of the emperor would render of such importance, and from which they could pour on the enemy, in his precipitate flight. In one place, they spoke of the loss of the heroes Bessieres and Duroc, who found, in the field of honour, a glorious death. In another, they calculated the advantageous consequences which the days of Lutzen and Bautzen must produce upon the campaign, opened with such splendour.

When these ideas of war and of ambition, kindled in the minds of the troops, by the unexpected news they had received, began to subside, they indulged in milder reflections; their hearts became softened by the hope of an approaching peace, which would again open to them the road to their beloved country, and restore so many thousand soldiers to their families, their property, and to all the beloved objects of their secret affections. Although General Rapp shared in those pleasing hopes, he could not remove from his mind the possibility of a renewal of hostilities.

On this supposition, all the works which a prolongation of the war required, were continued. He took advantage of the quiet of the armistice, which was to be continued from the 10th of June to the 25th of August, to arrange the different branches of the military administration, and to fortify the ramparts in those points that were weakest, which, although certainly not authorised by the laws of war, which forbid any addition to entrenchments or fortifications during an armistice, yet were the necessary consequences of the conduct of the Russians, who made new works round the place.

Quickly indeed did a variety of disagreeable symptoms, uncertain alarms, and the reserve the enemy maintained with the garrison, prove that these precautionary measures were not superfluous, and that the proceedings of the Congress at Prague did not promise a favourable termination.

The prospect of a new siege did not shake the fortitude of the French; and they proved, by the most energetic and determined measures, that they were prepared to brave the most awful crisis of the war. Nearly three-fourths of the troops had been carried off by pestilence and the sword; a crowd of officers, without soldiers to command, and consequently without any fixed duty to perform, remained. Those officers, to the number of sixteen hundred, desirous of giving a new proof of their willingness to devote themselves to the defence of the city, by an active and continued service, required permission to serve as private soldiers, and, formed into a chosen regiment, became an invincible and sacred phalanx; animated by honour, and enlightened by a martial spirit, they presented a model of the most admirable discipline, and military precision.

To their care was particularly confided the guard of the magazines, the hospitals, gates of the city, the maintenance of public order; and, when required, they were to act as a reserve, on whose heroism the last hopes of the battle might depend. The officers of engineers and artillery used every exertion to add to the fortifications of Dantzic; several redoubts were raised in advance of the city, to which the governor gave the names of his friends and companions, who had fallen in the field of battle; the chief redoubts were named Montebello, Gudin, Frioul, and Istria. Among the severe measures which the anticipation of hostilities suggested for the defence of Dantzic, there was one, which the example of every nation and every place justifies, but which was not the less cruel and afflicting to humanity.

The besieged dreading a famine, drove from the city four hundred foundlings, and ten thousand persons, whose indigence and total want of means compelled their banishment to be enforced in those moments of difficulty. The governor, and the officers of the garrison, lamenting the rigor an inflexible duty demanded, softened, by every aid in their power, the miseries of those unfortunate people, whom they were obliged to doom, on account of their poverty, to become wanderers through a country, ravaged and laid desolate by war.

The four hundred orphans, already so unfortunate in never having experienced the blessings of parental tenderness, spread themselves amongst the surrounding villages, sometimes repulsed by the inhabitants, whose hearts had become hardened by the horrors of war, and sometimes relieved by the pity their state excited. Thousands of poor people, who could not, like these forlorn children, claim the compassion particularly due to that weak and tender age, experienced the most bitter repulses; however, some found shelter in the Russian camp, whilst others were relieved in the city of Elbing; and it is a certain fact, that Providence did not suffer one to perish for want. The term of the armistice having expired, Napoleon refusing to accede to any arrangement on his part, which had for its basis any essential sacrifice; put an end to the Congress at Prague, using those presumptuous words, "*Aut Caesar aut nullus*," an alternative he could not have adopted without the most unfeeling temerity, nor even without the destruction of his own interests, from the distressed and exhausted state to which France was reduced, by his victories and his disasters.

The two months of tranquillity which Dantzic enjoyed in consequence of the armistice, divide the history of the siege of that city into two periods of equal duration, but totally distinct in the events they produced. In the first part of the siege, we have seen the miseries produced by an epidemic disease, and the constant but often unimportant assaults made by the besiegers, and the besieged, on their respective posts. In the second part, we shall witness the most sanguinary combats, both by land and sea; for months, by night and day, did the banks of the Baltic and Vistula resound without interruption with the thunder of a murderous artillery.

In the midst of conflagrations which threatened general devastation, and during the most frightful inundations, while famine decimated those whom disease had spared, and a bombardment left the finest parts of Dantzic a heap of ruins, upon those remains which the flames and waves seemed combined to destroy, in the midst of the ruins of a city bathed with so much blood, and consecrated by so many glorious deaths, with what admiration must we contemplate those heroes who stood at their posts immoveable and invincible; without weakness and without alarm, striking the very enemies that assailed them with admiration and astonishment!

The belligerent parties renewed hostilities with fresh advantages, which, stimulating their ardour, rendered the attack and defence of the place more dreadful, and on every side increased the scenes of carnage. The enemy, who had assembled eighty thousand men under the fortifications of Dantzic, was also assisted by an Anglo-Russian fleet, fifty sail of which cruised in the Baltic, at the mouth of the Vistula. The French had eight thousand men, who were divided into more than two hundred posts, but still the repose of the armistice had recruited their exhausted strength, and the most urgent wants of Dantzic had been relieved by the forage collected in the sorties from that city. Besides, what constituted the principal force of the French, what rendered them confident, bold, and invincible, was the expectation of being delivered by Napoleon.

The brilliant opening of the campaign of eighteen hundred and thirteen, the advantages of which were exaggerated, seemed to guarantee the future successes of the grand army. According to their suppositions, the triumphant course of the emperor would quickly extend itself to the extremities of Prussia. This hope frequently was productive of illusions; from the heights of the ramparts, the soldiers on duty would strain their eyes in gazing on the distant horizon, expecting to behold clouds of dust, announcing the approach of their companions. At night, they would listen with eager attention, in the hope of hearing the cannon of their emperor, which, according to an expression of that ambitious captain, resounded through the universe.

Meantime, the Russians had marked out their line of circumvallation; but with a precaution which disclosed the fears the former sorties of the besieged had caused, they opened their first trenches at the distance of nine hundred *toises* from Dantzic, an operation which appeared timid to the French, who, six years before, had attacked the same city, and opened their first parallel only three hundred *toises* distant from its walls. Yet every measure which may spare the effusion of human blood merits our praise; and besides, the Russians here united bravery to prudence, as they proved in the attack which they commenced on the 27th of August.

Amongst the positions which they most earnestly desired to make themselves masters of, were two heights of the utmost importance to the besieged. One called the Belvidere, because from its summit a lovely view of the city and surrounding country was discovered, if possessed by the enemy, would render him master of the suburbs of Langfuhr; the other, still more important, was the post of L'Etoile, which commands the suburbs of Ohra. From this position, the very interior parts of Dantzic were overlooked, and from this formidable fortification the city itself could be easily annihilated.

The French were so firmly assured of the immediate arrival of the grand army before the walls of Dantzic, that they supposed the design of the enemy to possess himself of the heights of Langfuhr and Ohra, was in order to defend the two roads by which they intended to make their retreat, and to hinder the besieged from annoying them, when raising the siege. This opinion rendered the garrison more daring in defending the post that had been attached, and on both sides there was an incredible carnage. The Russians, not satisfied with menacing the defences of Ohra and Belvidere, poured in on the city discharges of Congreve rockets, and on every point cannonaded the French advanced posts.

In order to disconcert those attempts, it was determined that a sortie should be made by a part of the garrison. General Husson saw, on his approach, that our first lines had given way before a numerous enemy; in an instant, he formed from the picked battalion of the ninth demi-brigade a close column, which pushed on at the *pas de charge*, on the wood of Ohra, and regained that position; at the same time the troops of Major Schneider, availing themselves of their success, rushed with fixed bayonets on the Russians, whom they drove from the different points where they had established themselves. Whilst those important movements were executing, in accomplishing which the brave Aide de Camp Besancon expired covered with wounds; and the Chiefs of Battalion D'Ellambert, Dupray Bellanger, and the brave Major Glieze were wounded; the cavalry of the garrison, supported by the infantry, advanced under the orders of Generals Cavaignac, and Farine, and pushed back the besiegers on their line of circumvallation; the cavalry burning with ardour drove the enemy before them into their trenches, which were filled with the slaughter that took place.

The contest now became dreadful; the Prince D'Aremberg, whose wounds, received in the campaign of Moscow, were not yet closed, had three horses killed under him; that brave and noble officer had the grief to behold his intimate friend, and *eleve*, the interesting Cinturione, perish by his side, in the flower of his age. This admired youth, a page to the Emperor Napoleon, sprung from a family which gave *doges* to ancient Liguria, had only a few days before received the rank of sub-lieutenant, and in this engagement fought for the first time, at the head of his troop; he was the pride and hope of his parents, and scarcely had attained his sixteenth year, when he fell far from his own mild and genial clime, near the shores of the tempestuous Baltic.

From Ohra to the post of Heubude, the fighting raged on every side; night itself could not terminate the attacks; whilst the combatants were engaged in various different places, under the walls of Dantzic, a freezing wind blew along the banks of the Vistula, and a cold rain fell in torrents; yet it was the month of August, a season generally burning in those northern climates, where the summers, although short,

are warm; a little while before, the heat of the day was insupport-
able; and now, by an extraordinary revolution in the atmosphere, the
disorder and confusion of the elements were mingled with the fury
of the combatants. In vain were the efforts of the Russians directed,
almost solely against the positions of Belvidere and Ohra; the French
remained masters of them, and every approach to those posts was covered with heaps of the enemy's slain; the next day, however, the enemy
again endeavoured to gain possession of them.

Ten thousand Russians advanced in good order against Belvidere,
and endeavoured to scale the fortifications; they were repulsed, and
again returned to the charge, a second time fell back, and once more
rushed forward, besieging with so much obstinacy, and such an immense number of troops, this important height, that General Rapp,
unwilling to sacrifice his troops in defence of a post, which, for so
many days, had cost such invaluable blood, and which it would be
impossible hereafter to preserve, gave orders to evacuate it.

As the post of Belvidere gave the Russians the command of Langfuhr, they only wanted now to possess themselves of the fortified
houses in the suburb, where three hundred Bavarian and Westphalian
troops had strongly barricaded themselves. While the enemy made in
vain the most serious efforts to conquer the resistance made in Langfuhr, the fury of his attacks against the redoubts of L'Etoile, Schidlitz,
and Stoltzenburgh, was not abated; but on no one of these different
points was his valour crowned with success. Exasperated at the determined resistance they had experienced, the Russians endeavoured to
force the French, by setting fire to the surrounding houses, to fall back
on the walls of Dantzic, and re-enter that city.

It was now night, and thousands of Cossacks wheeling round huge
masses of infantry, appeared, bearing in one hand a lance, in the other
a lighted torch. The village of Zikankenberg appeared first in flames.
This village, built on a hill, had been before deserted by its inhabitants,
and no cry was beard to interrupt its silent conflagration; but in Langfuhr it was otherwise; there the inhabitants, chased from their burning
roofs, strove to save themselves from the flames, and to carry off what
they could from the wreck of their property, almost wholly lost to
them forever. The distracted crowd flew to seek an asylum with the
inhabitants of Schidlitz and Stoltzenburgh; but whilst they pursued
their way towards those suburbs, flames appeared on every side, and
women, children, and old men, uttering the most piercing cries, and
spreading themselves around the country, were met by the fugitives

38

from the other burning villages; all those wandering and wretched people, mingling their griefs and distraction together, increased the horror and confusion of the dreadful scene; but still, they hoped to find a shelter from the dangers that pursued them, in Schellmull, and the village of Heubude; they turned that way, but the fire had got before them, and rapidly communicated from the one to the other of those places.

On every side, fire, carnage, and death were beheld; from every quarter the ear was assailed with the noise of burning houses, and clashing of arms; a population reduced to indigence and despair, without habitation or food, intermingled with hordes of savage troops, completed the horrors of this frightful siege. From the heights of the ramparts, the inhabitants of the interior of the city beheld, in awful silence, the horrible spectacle before them; for more than a league around, villages and separate houses were burning with fury, and threw so clear a light on the surrounding fields, that the very children could be distinguished accompanying their mothers in their flight— the heavens were as red as fire, and the surrounding waters seemed to roll with flames. Meantime, the three hundred Westphalian and Bavarian troops defended the fortified houses of Langfuhr; surrounded by smoking ruins, and an outrageous enemy, they rejected and repulsed every summons to surrender their post, in which they remained immoveable.

The governor, on being acquainted with their imminent danger, wished to relieve them, notwithstanding the difficulties of a sortie: the troops he sent to defend and rescue them from their perilous situation, on seeing the houses surrounded by flames, and on every side heaps of slain, supposed their companions had perished, and that it would be useless to seek them in the midst of a conflagration, which left no hope of safety for those it had so totally enveloped. They then re-entered the place, spreading consternation at the intelligence they communicated. The governor and garrison, with the most lively feeling, regretted the loss of those brave men, who were so valuable to them by their numbers, and so endeared to them by their courage.

The following morning, the garrison was as yet discoursing with sadness on the fate of their friends, when about sunrise these heroes were beheld advancing in good order towards the gates of the city. Those brave men had almost miraculously escaped from the circle of fire which surrounded them; they forced a passage through the piles of burning rubbish which encompassed them, and, having cut their way through the Russian battalions, arrived in the city: it would be impossible to express the joy their unhoped for return diffused through the garrison; on every side they were welcomed, with all the demonstrations that the most lively and fraternal friendship could suggest.

The bands of the different regiments in the city came out to meet them, and escorted them to the governor's palace, who loaded them with praises and rewards, caused all the wounded to be treated with the greatest care, and had them lodged in his own apartments. But fire was only a partial cause of the havoc experienced in the suburbs of Dantzic; an element not less destructive was in its turn to make known its dreadful power; to the utter surprise of the inhabitants of the country, who never, in any season, had experienced such a misfortune, without any apparent cause, the Vistula on a sudden rose to an extraordinary height; it overflowed its bed, and, joining its waters to those of the Radaune and the Mottlau, poured into the surrounding lakes, and, reaching the inundations to the north of the city, all those waters united, formed a dreadful abyss, vast and profound; this awful sea rushed foaming over the smoking ruins of the burning suburbs, and, more irresistible than the battering-rams of ancient days, beat down, with its mighty waves, the redoubts and fortifications opposed to it, forced into every quarter, inundated the streets, and obliged the citizens from every side to seek refuge in the tops of their houses, from whence they could only be saved by boats.

The bridges were swept away, nor could the dykes resist the fury of this outrageous element; the *palisadoes* of the fine forts, Napoleon and Lacoste, were carried off, and on every side earth and buildings disappeared. This sudden addition to their misery threw the inhabitants into total despair; and although fire, famine and disease, might have been supposed to have brought their wretchedness to a climax, yet this new and horrible addition to their misfortunes found, in their grief, new expressions to pourtray its horrors.

The inundations of winter, frightful as they are, appear less dreadful in that season, when hurricanes and tempests provoke such excesses; but in the month of August, in a temperate climate, contrary to every astronomical calculation, this scourge appeared the more fatal, as it seemed in opposition to the laws of nature, and that it was impossible to calculate its duration or results. This inundation lasted fifteen days, during which space the Anglo-Russian fleet bombarded the[1] forts of

---

1. These two forts are situated at the mouth of the Vistula one at the right, the other at the left.

Fahrvasser and Weichsulmunde, and, within the space of three days and nights, fired five hundred thousand shot of every calibre. Colonel Rousselot, who commanded those forts, remained tranquil, amidst this shower of balls and bombs. The Russians still persisted in their attacks upon the post of Ohra; it was from the heights of that position they wished to cannonade the city.

Every morning they sent five thousand men to try to escalade the post of L'Etoile; those troops fought during the day and night, and were then replaced by soldiers refreshed by sleep, and nourishing food. This post, so vigorously assailed, was defended by only six hundred men, fatigued by want of rest, and privations of every kind; but who, notwithstanding, maintained themselves in it for a month and an half, always repulsing the Russians, and performing prodigies of valour, under the command of Majors Dauger, Treny, and Schneider. On the tenth of August, the besiegers showed themselves determined, at last, to make the greatest sacrifices to obtain possession of the different points they had so long menaced in vain; at seven o'clock in the evening, they made a general attack on the posts of Schidlitz, Stoltzenburgh, and Ohra.

At the same time they threw thousands of fire-rockets into the city; these pernicious engines of destruction, whose progress was watched by the inhabitants, in the hope of interrupting their effects, fell in great quantities upon one of the hospitals of the place, and by a remarkable chance, which seemed to punish the besiegers, for having employed an invention almost as fatal as the Grecian fire of old, this hospital contained the Russian prisoners; but the garrison displayed no less eagerness on that account, to rescue those unfortunate; no longer did they consider them as their enemies, or as friends to those with whom they fought; placed under the tutelary guarantee of misfortune, which, amongst the brave and good, unites those whom fortune has separated, they met with the most generous assistance, and were astonished at being preserved, by their enemies, from that cruel death, to which their fellow-soldiers and countrymen had exposed them.

The flames consumed the entire of the edifice; the falling of a wall permitted a view into the interior of this receptacle of human woes, infirmity and suffering; the fire was seen rapidly to gain on the different beds of straw, from whence the sick, making a last effort to escape from the pursuit of a furious conflagration, saved themselves, pale, meagre and worn down, wrapped in the tattered remains of their clothes; the ceilings giving way, the staircases were exposed to view, crowded with sick and wounded Russians, leaning on French soldiers, who, at the hazard of their own lives, snatched them from the dreadful death which awaited them.

Whilst those events were taking place in the middle of the city, a part of the garrison was fighting without the walls. The posts of La Coupure and of La Barriere, in the suburb of Schidlitz, bad been forced by the enemy; the Chief of Battalion M. Carre came up with some troops, and retook one of them, but while he endeavoured to regain the other, the redoubled noise of artillery announced that an impetuous attack had been directed upon the most important points of Ohra. In fact, four thousand Russians, commanded by General Koulabakin, attempted with great boldness to climb the heights of L'Etoile, and force a passage into the neighbouring redoubts. Major Le Gros, with six hundred men, a number insufficient to guard so many positions, defended himself on this side, upon a number of points.

The post of L'Etoile was, however, gained possession of by the enemy, as was also the post Du Capitaine. At midnight, Major Le Gros received a reinforcement of a thousand soldiers, and General Husson having skilfully divided them, made the different detachments act with such concert, that the French simultaneously marched forward, with shouts of victory, drove the Russians from all the positions they momentarily occupied, and those whom they could not overtake were cannonaded in the fields, by the batteries of Stadgebiet and Frioul.

The Russians made in several parts a lively resistance, and defended themselves with bravery against the fire of the besieged. Major Dauger had his clothes pierced with balls, yet remained unhurt in the midst of one hundred and fifty French officers and soldiers, killed and wounded around him. The ground which the defenders of Dantzic had preserved, after a battle which had continued from eight o'clock in the evening until ten the next morning was covered with the enemy's slain; but when they hoped that so many fruitless attempts had discouraged the Russians, and a part of the French, after such a brilliant defence, had re-entered the city, the besiegers almost immediately returned with fresh troops to attack the post of Ohra, where there were only five hundred men.

The governor might have been able to send off an immediate reinforcement to this place; but with that prudence, which no less than bravery, directed his actions, he felt that the chosen troops of his garrison would sink by degrees under these reiterated assaults, and that the enemy, who could with ease repair his losses, would in the end gain possession of the works; he therefore deemed it better to abandon them entirely, than to sacrifice the lives of so many brave men, whose services were particularly required to defend the ramparts and walls of the city. Our soldiers, therefore, retired, but terrible in their retreat, they made a murderous fire across the *palisadoes*, and more than eight hundred Russians remained on the field of battle.

The enemy possessed themselves with joy of those eminences so ardently disputed for three months, and which had been so often moistened by rivulets of their blood; but they considered themselves rewarded for all their efforts, and recompensed for their losses, when they beheld, from the post of L'Etoile, the inner part of Dantzic and its environs laid open, and could direct their batteries against any point they pleased. But what cries of distraction and grief were heard from the houses in Dantzic, when the citizens, turning their affrighted eyes towards the summits of Ohra, pale and trembling, beheld those formidable bulwarks now become the points of attack, from whence the besiegers would be enabled to crush and batter down their walls. The suspended sword of Dionysius was less awful to the parasite of that tyrant, than the sight of those warlike engines drawn out on the heights of Ohra, to beat down Dantzic, and reduce it to ashes, unless the French consented to surrender.

The citizens of that place knew too well the inflexible courage of their hosts; they had too much experience of their immoveable constancy, to hope that a surrender would save the remains of a wretched population from the evils that threatened them, for a cause to which they were strangers, or rather a cause they detested, and which, notwithstanding, they were obliged to make sacrifices to support, that could scarcely be expected from the most devoted attachment. The Russians made immense preparations for the bombardment of the place; they burned all the surrounding houses, in order to unmask the city, and give a freer scope to the fury of their artillery; they at the same time fortified themselves in the positions they had with such difficulty gained, in order to assure their certain possession.

While they raised different works, and multiplied their redoubts, they put in requisition through the adjoining towns, all the working horses, who were incessantly employed in carrying balls, bombs, and artillery, in such immense quantities to these heights, scarcely accessible, that thousands of horses perished from fatigue. The Russians supposed the garrison reduced to a state of such wretchedness, as would induce them to receive any offers made to them with avidity. They pressed them to desert, promising them provisions, clothes, money, and every possible encouragement. The French were deaf to their seductions, and the example of their firmness had a powerful effect on the auxiliary troops, although they did not consider themselves bound by such a rigorous sense of duty to the service of France.

The Russians had then recourse to means more efficacious; they knew that the garrison was composed partly of Bavarians, and soldiers from other parts of Germany; they thought they could fix their determination to desert, by making it appear a lawful, if not an honourable duty, to return in the name of their country, their sovereigns, and fellow-citizens, who were now at war with Napoleon. For this purpose, they threw in amongst the advanced posts, bulletins, manifestoes, and proclamations, which announced the occupation of Westphalia, the rupture of Bavaria and Wurtemberg, with France, and a crowd of similar events, most likely to induce the Germans belonging to the garrison of Dantzic to escape from a place, where a longer stay would, in some degree, place them in a state of rebellion against their own governments.

To these proclamations, and many others addressed to the Poles, Neapolitans, and even to the French themselves, were annexed the reports by the Prince of Schwartzenberg, the Prince Royal of Sweden, and Marshal Blucher, of the victories gained in Bohemia, Prussia, Silesia, and Saxony. Notwithstanding the orders of the governor were, to burn those placards before they could be read, they came to the knowledge of many of the soldiers at the advanced posts, and, in spite of every precaution, their contents were circulated amongst the garrison; by some, received with indifference; by others, with consideration; and producing in their first effects a kind of distrust, which rendered the officers cautious in employing the Germans.

Almost every morning it was perceived, at either one post or another, that someone of the foreign troops had deserted. The strength of the garrison was by these means impaired, while the numbers of the enemy were increased, and the most alarming apprehensions were entertained, that traitors and spies might be in the interior of the city. Yet it must be allowed, to the honour of the foreign troops, who were united with the French for the defence of Dantzic, that if a few amongst them, after the orders which had been intimated to them, in the name of their sovereigns, quitted the garrison, yet to the last moment they did not cease to give proofs of their bravery and fidelity; nor did they ever give up any of the posts confided to their care..

As to the others, who formed the greater part, they refused constantly to abandon the French, to whom they were strongly attached by having participated for more than a year in their greatest misfortunes, and most dangerous enterprises.

There is, in adversity, a kind of sacred fellowship, an attractive and seducing power, which those who have not been associates and fellow-sufferers, for a length of time, with the unfortunate, cannot suppose. It cannot, besides, be denied, that the French soldier, by his manner, character, and temper, easily accommodates himself to the taste of others: sprightly and animated even in the midst of misfortunes, exciting admiration by extraordinary valour, inspiring gaiety by pleasant thoughts, and familiarly associating with the inhabitant of the North or South, he is a good and brave companion, prompt to assist, easy of access, uniting the open manners of the military man with the elegant politeness of the gentleman.

The Russians incessantly laboured to raise their batteries on the post of L'Etoile, and although they were greatly disturbed by the balls which were directed against them from the redoubts of Frioul and Bischoffberg, they were able to complete those fatal works. On the 20th of October, they fired an immense quantity of howitzers, cannon, and bombs, on the city and its environs; towards evening, a red hot ball fell in the middle of the place, and immediately a violent fire burst forth; the *generale* was beat, the troops flew to the spot, and the inhabitants assisted to stop the progress of the flames.

It was not now as it had been in the first conflagration, merely the destruction of deserted houses, or isolated villages; the magazines were now burning, where the garrison had lodged their only hopes of future subsistence; the buildings, in which were heaped up the riches and valuable property of Dantzic; those invaluable depots, where the traders had deposited their merchandise; in fact, the city itself, buildings and inhabitants, were threatened with destruction from the devouring flames, whose prodigious fury was increased by heaps of combustible matter, enormous piles of ship timber, firs, deals, and magazines of hemp; yet, by the most enthusiastic exertions, labour, and activity, the garrison was able to preserve the French magazines; and, by using fire-engines, served without distinction, by the soldiers, citizens, and even the general officers, they succeeded in extinguishing this dreadful fire.

The attempt which the enemy had made from the batteries of Ohra, encouraged him to continue the bombardment. His artillery was principally directed against those quarters where the garrison had established their principal magazines; bombs and red hot balls were constantly passing through the air; the artillery of the ramparts answered with fury to this bombardment, and fired regularly three thousand cannon shot within the twenty-four hours: each day, the Russians opened new batteries, which played pot only on the city, but on the redoubts which protected the approaches to it, and on the very last posts the besieged retained without the walls. By these means, they were enabled to command, on the heights of Schidlitz, the position the French as yet retained in that suburb, and to pierce every part of the works of Stoltzenburgh and the redoubt of Frioul with balls.

As to the suburb of Ohra, which was overlooked by the post of L'Etoile, the sides and summit of which were covered with artillery, there was not a single house left entire; and yet, although the besiegers were in possession of almost all the surrounding heights, from which they showered down canister shot upon the French posts, yet they were defended with the greatest *sang-froid* and bravery; and at times the enemy was attacked with success in his positions, and purchased dearly their possession. On the 27th of October, at midnight, the Russians, who had possessed themselves of all the posts of Schidlitz and Stoltzenburgh, were repulsed by the Chief of Battalion Carre; under the orders of that officer, the intrepid Captain Le Clerc drove the besiegers from the barrier of Schidlitz.

Three times the enemy retook, and as often was beat out of the post of Pichon. At the point of day, the French had retaken the positions they had occupied the day before, with the exception of those works the Russians had destroyed, despairing any longer to hold them against such an enemy. In the meantime, the bombardment of Dantzic kindled in that unfortunate city a new fire, more rapid and disastrous than the former one. While the troops of the garrison were endeavouring to extinguish it, the enemy, with the intention of causing a diversion, which would deprive the place of such assistance as might save it from total destruction, made an impetuous attack, and gained possession of the advanced works of the redoubt Frioul, where fifty men chose rather to perish than surrender!—and, as a part of the garrison made a sortie to regain this important post, and to drive the enemy from the ramparts, the fire, left, unrestrained, to exercise all its fury, caused the most frightful disasters.

The magazines, where the besieged had preserved their last resources, were quickly consumed; and the burning roofs of these vast edifices falling in, buried under their ruins the inestimable heaps of flour and corn which had been preserved, and left the city a prey to all the horrors of famine. It would be impossible for the imagination to depict the horrible situation of the feeble garrison of Dantzic, which fifty thousand men, assisted by fire in every shape, attacked without relaxation: a prey to the miseries of their present situation, yet were their future prospects still more gloomy and frightful. To make head against the multitude of dangers, which all at once assailed them, our soldiers were only relieved from one post, to march to another; nor could they find repose after the fatigues of a sortie, before they were obliged to sustain the fury of an assault; fighting during the day under the burning heat of a summer's sun; in the night, by the light of the flames; they only quitted their arms, to go and repair the dykes, broken down by irruptions of the sea, or to extinguish fires, bursting out in different places, from the falling bombs and Congreve rockets.

And yet, to sooth and alleviate their misery, the hope of a speedy deliverance was denied them; the salutes of artillery, which announced in the Russian camp the victories of the Coalesced Powers, the official reports, and the information of some confidential persons, who gave details of these advantages, too plainly taught the garrison, that no choice was left but captivity or death. But, to fill up the measure of the distresses of the besieged, to complete the evils they had to endure, that nothing should be wanting to the glory of their defence, they were doomed to experience the extreme rigours of famine. The provisions had been nearly exhausted; for some time only horses and domestic animals remained; and the distributions, which were every day made with the most rigid economy, having been supplied from the magazines which were consumed, the besieged were deprived of every means of subsistence.

The citizens of Dantzic, sacrificed to the defence of the place, experienced still more severely these cruel privations; yet the burning of the magazines, belonging to the garrison, was in some degree of service to them; for these wretched people, perishing for want of food, spread themselves on every side, like voracious animals, upon the smoking ruins of the public buildings, where they dug up from amongst the burning ashes, provisions half consumed by the flames, and thus found the means of prolonging life in the bosom of destruction. In this situation so deplorable, when existence appeared a burden almost too heavy to bear, the besieged, called every hour by the sound of the *generale*, were obliged to defend the ramparts and advanced posts, there to engage with a robust enemy, not enervated by disease, and who received in his camp abundance of every kind of provisions from the neighbouring countries, and people now friendly to the cause of the Coalesced Powers.

But at the moment when the defenders of Dantzic, physically exhausted by absolute want, and warlike vigils, appeared no longer capable of resistance, they gave a proof of daring boldness, which would seem surprising in warriors whom reverses had not overwhelmed, and whose enterprises had never been counteracted by misfortune. The besieged formed the idea of selecting out of the whole garrison *one hundred men,* whose pre-eminent intrepidity was indisputably allowed, and whose constancy and calmness, in the midst of dangers, had been universally acknowledged. These heroes, chosen from amongst the brave, formed a band, which they called the Free Company, and devoted themselves to actions the most rash and dangerous. According to the regulations of their association, they were bound to surprise at night the enemy's posts, to introduce themselves into their camps, to carry off their chiefs and generals, even in the midst of their tents and guards, to destroy the works of the besiegers under the very fire of the batteries, to spike their artillery, intercept their convoys, and, in a word, to make the most desperate and decisive attempts.

The heroes of this self-devoted corps would recall to our recollection the remembrance of those haughty Arabs, who, at the command of the old man of the mountain, thought themselves happy in going to brave inevitable death, by striking their victims, in the middle of the mighty armies which the east and west then poured forth; if we could rank men, whose souls were inspired by the love of glory, with those fanatic disciples of a crafty impostor. The first achievement of the Free Company equalled the expectation its institution excited.

As soon as the shades of night had enveloped the surrounding country, our hundred heroes embarked in light skiffs at the mouth of the Vistula, and silently coasted along those banks, where, in former days, adventurers as daring as themselves, those piratical kings and warriors of Scandinavia, sailed along to visit those fortresses, bathed by the mighty waves of the Baltic and Northern Ocean, to seek for adventures of love or war. At midnight, the Free Company landed at the village of Bousac, occupied by two thousand of the enemy's troops. Having put the sentinels to death, they made a dreadful slaughter of all the soldiers they could meet, burned the magazines, destroyed a part of the artillery, and, loaded with booty, returned to the banks of the river; but a sudden squall had driven off their *barks*, which, tossed by the winds, floated far from the reach of those heroes.

Deprived of a passage by water, they had no other resource but to regain by land the walls of Dantzic, across a number of leagues of country, covered with Russian armies, who closed up every avenue. But those men, endowed with courage superior to the greatest perils, had vowed to encounter every obstacle. They marched all night over a hostile country, beset with dangers and difficulties; in one place, they had to fight with detachments of the enemy's forces, scattered through the fields; in another, they had by stratagem to pass through numerous battalions; they had rocks to climb, rivers to cross, and entrenchments and barriers to scale; yet, after performing deeds which are almost incredible, they entered the city at eight o'clock in the morning, where their fellow-soldiers listened with avidity to the romantic recital of their glorious career. It has been already related, that during the fire in Dantzic, the enemy had attacked the redoubts of that place, and that part of the garrison had made a sortie to protect them; here again the exploits of the Free Company claim our admiration.

The hundred warriors who composed it, supported by one hundred more soldiers, wished to retake from the Russians the advanced past of the redoubt Frioul, of which they had gained possession; they silently marched to the foot of this post, climbed up the heights, and darting over the *pallisadoes*, shewed themselves at once to the astonished enemy; one hundred and fifty men were put to the sword, the remainder were made prisoners. After this signal advantage, and the success obtained to the north of the city, where a murderous fire of musquetry swept off entire ranks of the enemy, Count Heudelet gave orders that these harassed troops should return into the city, when the sound of arms, shouting and cries, announced to him, that the French were seriously engaged towards Schidlitz and Stoltzenburgh.

It was one o'clock in the morning, and no objects could be distinguished but by the light of houses burning here and there over the country, or where a momentary gleam appeared from the streams of fire, which marked the course of the Congreve rockets through the air. Count Heudelet was informed, that the besieged were repulsed in these two suburbs, and that they had retreated under the protection of the neighbouring batteries. The general immediately sent to require from the city all the disposable troops, and at the same tine ordered the first demi-brigade to march out of the fortress of Bischoffberg. These forces formed a junction, but the darkness of the night was so great, that Generals Heudelet and Grandjean, not being able to form an opinion of the number or position of the enemy, waited until the break of day, that they might act with more precision and effect. As soon as the dawn of morning had thrown a feeble light over the country, General De Villiers received orders to retake the post on the right of Schidlitz, which the enemy had obtained; and General Breissand was directed to march into Schidlitz and Stoltzenburgh, and to draw up before the fort of Bischoffberg. General Breissand marched forward, and drove the enemy from the trenches he had made during the night, upon an extent of two hundred *toises*, on a parallel with the fort of Bischoffberg, and retook all the posts they had occupied; but the Russians, considerably reinforced attacked General Breissand; that able officer was to have been supported by General De Villiers, but the length and difficulty of the roads retarded his progress, and exposed General Breissand's corps alone to the enemy's attack.

His situation did not alarm him; he ordered a general charge, and the engagement begun. In a moment after, General De Villiers attacked, and carried by main force the posts to the right; the Russians were repulsed from the plain of Stoltzenburgh; but, in the moment of his success, the brave General Breissand was mortally wounded; to replace him, General Heudelet sent the Chief of his Staff, Colonel Quesnel; that officer, full of enthusiasm, activity and honour, possessed, in an eminent degree, the power of exciting the ardour of his companions in arms, by the example of his valour and the eloquence of his language; although as yet young, he had seen fifteen years of active service, and, by his noble and daring conduct during the siege, added lustre to the military reputation he had before acquired, in the Campaigns of Italy, Spain, and the North.

The Russians abandoned the posts of Schidlitz and Stoltzenburgh, to the brilliant boldness of our troops, but on the following day they threw themselves on the latter suburb, with eight hundred men; seventy French troops, who defended it, retreated to the gates of Schidlitz. General Husson perceiving this retrograde movement, drew two hundred and eighty men from different positions, at whose head he rushed on Stoltzenburgh, but he was suddenly stopped by a long and deep trench, which the enemy had hastily dug up, and furnished with numerous troops, protected by artillery. Those obstacles were insurmountable, and the general was obliged to retire under the Fort of Bischoffberg, towards which the Russians began immediately to carry on their trenches.

The governor perceived that it would be useless to persist in re-taking posts, which the enemy, six times more numerous, attacked without respite; he, therefore, left only a cordon of troops round the city, to observe the manoeuvres of the besiegers, and to disturb their advanced posts, by a continued fire of musketry, and perpetual skirmishing. Meantime, famine was wasting away the garrison and citizens of Dantzic. The most vile and disgusting food was bought at an enormous price, and devoured with avidity.

Every morning hand-barrows were employed to carry off those unfortunate people, who perished in the streets through absolute want; but without detailing those dreadful scenes of horror and despair, the imagination may conceive what was the situation of Dantzic, when two women were taken up for selling human flesh,[2] and it was deemed cruel in the governor to put a stop to this infernal traffic. Nor can it hardly he supposed, that after an engagement it was found necessary to inter the dead, to save their bodies from the voracity of the besieged, who eagerly strove to seize on this execrable food! It was in such a state of misery, when a single house did not remain in the city, which had not been ravaged by fire, or injured by bombs or balls, that the Senate of Dantzic, in the hope of saving the inhabitants from total destruction and despair, presented the following address to Count Rapp.

Sir,

All Europe bears testimony to your exploits; Victory has called you from the frozen summit of the Alps to the burning sands of Egypt, from the borders of the Nile to the banks of the Danube and the Spree, and from the fields watered by the Tagus to the shores of the Baltic. Your name, Sir, is connected with all the successes, which, for twenty-five years, have attended the French arms; and your eighteen wounds are witnesses, that you have been ever ready to sacrifice your life to the duties of your noble profession. After having done so much for glory, will you not, Sir, deign to yield a little to the cause of humanity? for surely you cannot gather more laurels amidst those walls, where only the cypress is seen steeped in our blood, and bedewed with our tears.

The losses, the privations, the misfortunes of every kind, we have borne with patience and resignation for your cause, allow us,

---

2. It was made up as sausages!

perhaps, the privilege of being favourably heard, at those critical moments, when our city is menaced with total destruction, should you longer determine to defend it. It is not from this siege we are to date our sufferings; a former siege, Sir, sustained against yourself, had already annihilated the prosperity of these countries; since that period, submissive to your government, we have repaid, by innumerable proofs of obedience, devotion and fidelity, the solemn promise made to us, to protect our industry, our commerce, and the independence of our laws. Yet for these six years, our port, once so flourishing, which opened to us the riches of a successful commerce, has been, by order of your sovereign, closed against those powers with whom he was at war. Our vessels have perished in this fatal inaction, our magazines are now no more opened to the chances of a lucrative exportation, and every source of our prosperity has decayed away.

Dantzic, fallen from its commercial rank, and deprived of the honours of its flag, has not remained less attached to France; although, instead of its counting-houses, its warehouses, and its pacific speculations, it only exhibits the appearance of a depot for arms, and immense preparations for war, to which we have contributed with all our means; and when, Sir, the elements conspired to destroy your grand army, dispersed its remains, and delivered them to an enemy emboldened by its disasters; when the people betrayed you in your passage, Dantzic remained faithful, and hastened, by an hospitable reception and disinterested cares to soften the sufferings, and sooth the disasters of your sick soldiers.

An epidemic disease met our generous efforts; and, without a murmur at the cause of our grief, we wept over twelve thousand of our fellow-citizens, who perished by contagion. This city was, in the mean time, besieged by the Russians, and your measures of defence called on our part for immense sacrifices; all private property was converted to public use; we possessed nothing we did not share, or rather exclusively deliver, to the urgent wants of your hospitals and your garrison; and yet. Sir, what complaints have we preferred, or what remonstrances have we made, during the long exercise of those destructive requisitions?

But, alas! Sir, these are but the smallest of our evils; for after having lost our fortunes, we still have banishment or death to dread. A part of the inhabitants of this mourning city were driven from their firesides, abandoned to the mercy of public pity; others, victims of the evils of a rigorous siege, regret that they were not included in that sad proscription. The Russians, after having burned down our suburbs, showered a destroying fire, and burning bails upon our city. The dykes which restrained the fury of the waves have been burst open the river which bathes our ramparts has sapped their shattered foundations, and opened a passage for its waves through our ruined habitations.

Even, Sir, at the moment we lay before you our miseries, forty batteries belonging to the enemy, directed day and night against the circle of our walls, vomit forth terror and death amongst us. The father is struck in the middle of his family, and often the entire family disappears amidst the crash of burning ruins, which engulf them in their fall. At every moment, new fires excite new alarms, and, in this eventful state, the living cannot reckon on a single day of existence.

Yet it is in vain that the remainder of our population hope to escape from the fatal explosion of the bomb, by flying for refuge to the subterraneous parts of our dwellings; another danger not less frightful pursues them. Famine, more horrible than any other evil, multiplies scenes of grief and rage, which the most inflexible Conqueror must shudder to behold. But no, the groans, the piercing shrikes, the last sighs of so many wretched beings, a prey to all the tortures of despair, and to the convulsions of a violent death, will not be lost to our cause!—they will eloquently plead for a dying people; you, Sir, will hear them, and you will save those victims, who yet survive so many scourged.

Do not fear, able and courageous general, that the surrender of those wails can betray irresolution; an heroic resistance for eleven months, perpetual combats, the fury of which, even night itself had not the power to suspend; actions and deeds, emulative of fabulous times would justify the necessity of the act, if it could require it.

Besides, Sir, it is not the power of the enemy that will reduce the city; it is not even to the force of disease, inundations, or famine, that you will have yielded our ramparts: no, Sir, our misfortunes, our tears, and our prayers alone, could have conquered you. Invincible to force, you will be subdued by pity;

and this one act of a feeling heart will raise a more splendid trophy to your fame, than all the victories you have gained.

Count Rapp heard this address, but he still persisted in the defence of the place.

The 11th of November, the Free Company issued from the city, at two hours after midnight, and precipitated themselves into the trench the enemy had dug before Wemberg; one hundred and forty Russians were put to the sword. Ten desperate enterprises of this kind were attempted with success by those brave and determined warriors, many amongst whom lost their lives. Lieutenant Connard was wounded in it for the twentieth time. M. Rosey gave, in the foremost ranks, proofs of the most extraordinary courage. From the 11th to the 28th of November, there were every day continued skirmishes, and an incessant cannonade kept up. Twenty batteries, armed with a hundred and twenty pieces of cannon, played continually on the post of Bischoffberg; all the other redoubts of the enemy were equally formidable.

The situation of the besieged now became such, that resistance became culpable, not only in the eyes of humanity, but according to the most rigorous principles of war; for the governor could no longer plead, in justification of his inflexibility, any of those motives which had at first engaged him to sustain the siege of Dantzic. He had defended that city because immense magazines had been deposited there, but which, the fire had totally consumed. It had been defended as a place of refuge for those soldiers who would have perished had they a longer march to sustain; but the greater part of those men had already lost their lives, and a capitulation was the only hope of safety left for the remainder. Its defence was undertaken in order to injure the enemy on his retreat, under the supposition that Napoleon would have been victorious; but, after the most serious conflicts, that captain had repassed the Rhine with the shattered remains of the grand army.

In such a state, what advantage could be proposed in a longer resistance? To preserve a heap of ruins and tombs; to annihilate the wretched inhabitants of a city, which owed to the French the calamities which overwhelmed it, and even to complete the destruction of the French themselves, without serving the cause of their emperor. Still less could it benefit their country, already too much afflicted by the loss of so many thousands of her children, fallen in the plains of Moscovy, Poland, Prussia, and Saxony. All those considerations, at length, prevailed in the mind of General Rapp, over a resolution which would have been fatal. The governor and his garrison had done all that could be expected from the most intrepid soldiers, and all that remained was to procure honourable terms.

The Convention concluded between His Royal Highness the Prince of Wurtemberg and Count Rapp, was in substance, that the plaice should be surrendered on the first of January, if it was not relieved before that period.

The garrison to march out with the honours of war.

That it should preserve six hundred pieces of artillery and all its baggage, and should return to France, under the condition of not serving against the Allies for a year and a day.

As soon as this Convention had been signed, the Prince of Wurtemberg demanded from the governor those soldiers of the garrison who belonged to the different Coalesced Powers. Count Rapp not having any motive to refuse, agreed to this claim; and, in consequence, the Bavarians and other foreigners, whose sovereigns had declared war against the Emperor Napoleon, separated from the French.

Their parting was affecting; those brave men vowed eternal esteem and friendship, which, they declared, no political dissensions should interrupt; they all embraced their companions on taking leave, and many exchanged swords. At the head of the Bavarians was Colonel Butler, an officer whose heart was the seat of every virtue that could adorn a soldier. Thus parted those valiant men, worthy of appreciating each other's merit; and, endeared by mutual esteem, they separated; and, faithful to the commands of their sovereigns, went to fight those, whose fellow-soldiers they had been.

Meantime, the French yielded to the hope of once more returning to their homes, and forgetting, in the bosom of their families, the misfortunes they had experienced. A few days only were to elapse, according to the regulations of the Convention, before they should pursue their route towards their beloved France: everyone was with delight making preparations, and only waited the expected signal; when the general received a letter from the headquarters of the Russians, which announced, that the Emperor Alexander had refused to ratify that article which allowed the French to return to France. That monarch demanded that they should be sent into Russia, as prisoners of war.

This intelligence shocked the French, who were at once, from the sweetest prospect hope could form, plunged into the most gloomy despair; for what alternative could be more dreadful than a severe captivity, amidst the frozen climes of Moscovy, and, after such indescribable fatigues, unexampled dangers and misfortunes, more almost than human strength was capable of supporting, to be obliged to march, during a rigorous season; and into these very countries where so many of their countrymen had perished, by the severity of a cold and inhospitable climate!

The idea of such a termination to their sufferings wounded the pride of the besieged; they formed the resolution of issuing out with arms in their hands, and dying upon the bodies of their enemies, whose sovereign had violated the laws of nations, and broken a treaty, to which a prince, his general, had subscribed his name. In the bitterness of adversity, and the anguish of despair, those severe complaints and insulting reproaches were not surprising. Yet the Russian monarch alleged, in justification of his refusal to ratify the convention, the conduct of Napoleon, who, in opposition to a similar treaty, signed with the garrison of Thorn, had compelled the soldiers who composed it to serve before the expiration of the time agreed on.

If such was the case, General Rapp and the garrison of Dantzic could only accuse their emperor himself, for the severe terms which formed the basis of a second capitulation; which, however, it was necessary to agree to, in order to stop the fury and arrest the vengeance of those soldiers who remained in the garrison, and, prompted by despair, determined to seek a period to their woes, at the point of the sword. But they had sufficiently proved how little they feared the greatest dangers; and, in their deplorable state, there was more bravery in supporting existence than in meeting death. They therefore marched out of the city, which had been almost beaten down around them, and, in quitting it, passed over an immense fosse, which had served as a cemetery daring the siege, and where above forty thousand bodies had been interred.

There for ever their friends reposed, whilst they set out, doomed to submit to a melancholy exile on the borders of the Nieper and the Volga. Yet they received from the inhabitants of those countries the most soothing attentions, and the most affecting testimonies of their kindness and benevolence. Even in those distant climes, the bravery and misfortunes of the defenders of Dantzic were known, and their renown inspired every breast with a veneration for those heroes, which rendered their misfortunes sacred. The people every where contended for the pleasure of affording them all those sweet and soothing consolations, which could soften or alleviate the sorrows of suffering captivity.

The return of the Bourbons, and of peace soon after, brought with them their freedom, and at last their expectations have not been deceived. Already they behold the rivers and hills of their beloved country; they once more revisit those beautiful fields, which plenty and the blessings of Heaven have covered with abundance, and which the devastations of war seem not to have sullied.

Intrepid Sons of France, you, whose daring deeds and unshaken constancy have been admired during a siege, in which Fortune exhausted on you all her vengeance, at length forget all your reverses and your sorrows, in the calm leisure of an all-healing peace; or rather preserve for ever the remembrance of the miseries and disasters which war had caused around you, in order to feel more impressively this maxim—*that however dazzling the illusive splendour may be, which surrounds the weighty trophies of the conqueror, a peaceful and paternal sovereign can alone constitute the happiness of his people.*

GENERAL JEAN RAPP

Jan Henryk Dabrowski

POLISH INFANTRY

POLISH LEGION

PONIATOWSKI

The Background & History of the
Siege of Dantzig, 1813
An Extract from 'Dantzig and Poland'

Contents

The Prussian Occupation

During the late 17th and early centuries a serious storm was gathering over Dantzig, a nearer peril from which there was no escape, a danger that might be averted for a time, but could not be escaped. It was the Prussian peril. The Prussian king, heir of the Teutonic Order, appeared as a candidate for the prey of four centuries ago, lost then by the knights.

For long enough the Hohenzollerns, one after the other, had paid passing visits at various times and had a look at Dantzig. On their accession to the throne, journeying from Berlin to the coronation city of Koenigsberg, they were wont to make a halt in that town, and though they were not yet able to lay a covetous hand upon it, they at least surveyed its riches and beauty with eager eyes. Thus the Great Elector, Frederic William, passed through in 1662. Frederic I passed through five times (1690, 1697-98, 1701), Frederic William I twice (1714, 1739). The latter used his opportunity to entice away for his suite some tall grenadiers of the city, who had been assigned to him as a guard of honour. Lastly Frederic the Great visited Dantzig four times, first as heir to the throne, and then as king (1735, 1740, 1753).

This last, most distinguished as well as most dangerous guest, did not indeed strive to carry out in person the design of seizing Dantzig. Nevertheless, he was to work out most precisely the plan of occupation, and start it on the way of direct and brutal execution. For long he had had his eye on the city, and desired it from the time when, as heir to the throne, he saw how it defended its beloved King Leszczynski. He wished to be loved by the people of Dantzig, and had his own peculiar way to compass this end. He wanted to be loved because of excessive hatred. He wanted the people so to hate mightily the enemy in him, that they would at last be forced rather to love in him the ruler. He wanted to strangle them so long as neighbours, that they would finally prefer to enjoy peace as his subjects.

This unexampled design of extortion on the part of Frederic the Great towards Dantzig, with all its refinement of detail, began with the first entrance into power of Poland's last king, Stanislaw August Poniatowski. From the king's election-day Frederic began ceaselessly to sap the strength of the defenceless Republic, and especially the city of Dantzig. Thus, under diverse pretexts, now temporary reprisals, now averred titles of overlordship, the Prussian king began to strangle the town cleverly and deliberately, and all with conscious consistency and calculated masterliness. As a first pretext he used the proclamation of universal tariffs by the Diet assembled at Warsaw 1764 for the election of Poniatowski. Although the matter was a purely internal one for Poland, and the tariff involved all her boundaries alike as well as her trade relations with all her neighbours, yet Frederic felt himself injured personally, and justified in making good the fancied wrong with his own hand, and according to his own sweet will. He made it good, of course, chiefly at the cost of Dantzig.

The city lived on its trade with Poland, thanks to the free course of the Vistula. Frederic established a station below Kwidzyn-Marienwerder, in the middle of the river; instituted unheard-of transit duties, introduced intolerable rights of search, planted his soldiers and set up his cannon (1765). Having thus pressed under his heavy hand the life-giving artery of the city, he began systematically to draw it tighter, without any mercy. It was plain robbery, but it brought Frederic in considerable returns. For this reason he paid no attention to the powerless protestations of the Republic of Poland and of Dantzig itself. Fortunately, intervention came from a stronger Power, that of Russia. Catherine II could not be deaf to the desperate complaints of the Polish King in this regard, since he had been elected under her aegis, and Poniatowski was her own candidate. As a result of her interposition Frederic had to yield, and remove his station in the Vistula, which brought him so much gold.

But matters endlessly greater soon came along, which thrust that of the tariff into a corner. Complications of a political and religious nature arose, of which the final outcome was the First Partition of the Republic. Frederic now put forth his whole skill, first as tempter, then as negotiator. At first his purpose was, either by pretences of favour, or by crushing them with unbearable oppression, to sever the people of Dantzig from Poland, to draw them toward himself, and to reconcile them to an occupation. His next purpose was, after getting to the point of negotiations for a partition, at the same time, and as a part of the treaty, to obtain Dantzig for his own possession as an addition to his other gains from the transaction.

He began then first to make overtures to the people of the city. At a time when he was kindling in Poland the question of religious dissension as a step toward the partition, the zealous Protestant king, who had just laid his tribute on the earnings of his fellow-believers the Protestant citizens of Dantzig by confiscating their wares, now began all at once with zealous energy to appear in the role of champion of their religious liberties against Polish fanaticism. And to attain his ends, he began in the name of the common Protestant faith to urge the people, through his clever agent in Dantzig, to link up with the Confederation of Dissidents in Poland.

The honest councillors of the city defended themselves against uninvited guardianship. They swore that their faith was suffering no wrong, that they had no need to complain of any of their burdens as Dissidents to the Polish Crown. Finally, and really under compulsion, they joined the Confederation as ordered; but in the moment of entry they entrenched themselves under the most express reservation, that "they do not commit themselves to anything which would compromise their loyalty owed to His Majesty the King of Poland, and to the Most Serene Republic" (1767).

A couple of years later, when the project of the partition was ripe, Frederic adopted other tactics toward Dantzig. From the role of seduction he returned to that of oppression; from being a gracious master to being tyrannizer. Under pretence of searching for deserters, he sent to the city recruiting contingents, and took by force from among the people recruits for the Prussian army. The unbounded deceit of these pretensions was evident to all. He insisted on taking four thousand conscripts who had "deserted" a scandalous pretence, which would have involved a fair part of the whole male population of the city. Using similar trumped-up claims, he placed Prussian regiments on the city's territory, and under the pretext of some recompense due to him he exacted a wholly arbitrary contribution from the inhabitants of 200,000 *ducats* (1770).

As executor of these crying injustices, he placed in Dantzig his agent, the notorious Legation-Councillor Junck, a professional thief and provocateur, about whom even a modern official Prussian historian had to admit that his chief business was "to provoke the people of Dantzig." Having exhausted these pretensions as to deserters and re-

71

cruits, Frederic, who was never at a loss for devices, thought out a new plan. With the beginning of the new year he invented an "epidemic "as a reason for investing the city with a hygienic "cordon" of troops, in return for which service he obliged the city to pay him during the two years 1771-72 100,000 *ducats.*

Meanwhile the negotiations proper began about the First Partition of Poland. From the start Frederic had his mind set on Polish Prussia, but he did not forget Dantzig. This neighbour and friend, the King of Prussia, the zealous *defensor fidei*, the uninvited champion of the Protestant faith of the people of Dantzig, as well as of their physical health, now graciously designed to express his willingness to receive them wholly beneath his sceptre.

It is true they were in no hurry to hasten under the wings of their fellow Protestant black eagle, for they knew very well his insatiable appetite for Customs dues. But Frederic insisted on converting them to the Prussian faith in his own way. And one must do him the justice to admit that he did not let any possibilities slip. Now he was fawning, now vehement, now menacing, but ever full of resources both in wealth of his tactics and in his eager persistency This greed and persistency struck his contemporaries forcibly. Voltaire remarked to him tauntingly that if the *Czarina* had thoughts of Byzantium and Athens, he did not cease thinking of Dantzig. "Your Royal Majesty would prefer the port of Dantzig to that of Piraeus: and rightly!"

Frederic went to work like a master. At the outset, when the first negotiations were on, he pretended to give up Dantzig entirely, reserving himself, of course, "suitable recompense for that city." Then, after assuring himself of quite plenteous "recompense" for a thing which did not belong to him at all, he began afresh to remember the city, this wondrous treasure, and that with increased vehemency. During the negotiations about the partition in St. Petersburg he kept urging his claim to get control of the city right to the end, before the principal mistress of the business, Catherine. He was bound to have from her adjudged that indispensable, trifling, addition of Dantzig to his share of Poland.

He wrote to his ambassador in St. Petersburg:

As far as Dantzig is concerned, I regard the matter as quite simple. Why, Avignon was once the Pope's, and the French took it. Strasbourg was a free city, and it was incorporated by Louis XIV. History shows many other such cases. For the rest I should not care about any such insignificant trading town. But one can see at a glance on the map that it cuts in two all my possessions.

He was deeply offended that "such a row is made" about poor "Dantzig, which would be only a nuisance (*une niaiserie*) to the Russians." He even threatened, if refused, to break his alliance with the Empress, taking advantage of her difficulties with the Turks, and frightening her with the threat of getting Austria to intervene. He wrote to St. Petersburg:

> I am a business man. Ye come to me to buy goods, to get help, and subsidies. I say. Please pay me so and so much, and in such coin. Ye reply. We do not wish to pay in this coin. In this case the merchant bows low, shuts up his wares, and prefers to betake himself elsewhere. How, then, my lords Russians! Do you want me to run risks? Do you want reinforcements from me? Agreed, but Polish Prussia and Dantzig—that is the price of my help! You see, my beloved Russians, you must decide whether you need my wares or not. Can you get along without them? Perhaps Dantzig, which you love so dearly, can give you what I am selling too dear. Indeed I find it hard to believe that such a vanity (*une misere*) as Dantzig is should detain for a moment the clear and wise mind of the great empress.

All this eloquence availed for the time being naught. It was premature. The unhappy Frederic could not yet reach Dantzig. The resistance of the people of the city themselves was naturally not insignificant; they defended themselves desperately against their hated Prussian neighbour. They raised an alarm throughout the whole of Europe. They turned for aid to their former trading comrades and patrons, the General Estates of Holland. They turned also for help to Great Britain.

We have noted that the relations of Dantzig with England were of very early date. Of yore England fed her people with Polish grain brought by way of Dantzig, supplied her fleet with magnificent timber for masts from Polish forests, and in return kept Poland provided with her fine cloths and the savoury products of her overseas colonies. In the days of Elizabeth George Carrew reached Dantzig as the Queen's special messenger, bearing a declaration of her favour and of her commercial preferences (1598). Dantzig in return sent an embassy to King James I.

It is true that at times passing disputes arising out of local commercial rivalries grew into fairly sharp quarrels between Dantzig and England; but they were arranged without difficulty to the satisfaction of both parties. The agreements made between the delegates of the English Company and the Senate of Dantzig led to a mutually helpful Commercial Treaty (1631). The men of Dantzig secured from Charles II an interpretation of the universal English Navigation Act, which gave them special advantages (1668). John Robinson, Envoy Extraordinary of Queen Anne, came to Dantzig, and concluded in her name an Anglo-Dantzig agreement, very advantageous to the city. Settled in 1706, it regulated mutual trade relations for the whole century, and has never been properly done away with to this very day.

It was just because of violence done to this last agreement by Frederic, that Dantzig turned with complaints to the English Government. At once the citizens set forth eloquently through the Polish Ambassador in London, Bukaty, the peril that hung over their town—not only of plundering, but even of seizure by Prussia. These exertions called forth at least a certain moral reaction. Bukaty's memorial, printed in English in London, drew the attention of the public. The young Edmund Burke time after time raised his voice against the violence being done to Poland, in his *Annual Register*, in the years 1772-73.

Frederic became uneasy. He tried through Maltzan, his Ambassador in London, to check the interest shown in Britain for Poland in general and Dantzig in particular. He wrote:

> England has no reason for worrying about Polish matters. They are really strange to her, and cannot have the least effect either upon her position or her interests.

Unfortunately, the then English Minister of Foreign Affairs, Lord Suffolk, rightly branded at a later time by the great Chatham as an "unconstitutional, inhuman and unchristian" politician, did not make a successful defence of Poland, which was being torn in pieces, nor yet of unhappy Dantzig, exposed as a victim of Frederic the Great's extortions. The bold and far-seeing writer J. Williams estimated better than the minister the unworthy conduct of the Prussian king, "whose family has received their all, except the lakes and sand banks of Brandenburg, from the Crown of Poland," and has never ceased to repay the Republic with the bitterest hatred and the gravest injuries.

In such a pass the people of Dantzig, who could not rely either on the help of powerless, plundered Poland, nor yet on the distant, platonic sympathy of Holland and England, once more appealed to the mighty and near-lying Russia. Here once more they did in fact find a certain temporary support. Of yore Czarina Anna had promised in a special amnesty (1736), after the city had been taken by Muennich, and the Dantzig delegation had begged for pardon in St. Petersburg, "her most serene intervention for maintaining the present rights and liberties of Dantzig, religious and other." Later, after the city had been forced to identify itself with the Confederation of Dissidents, the same decree was confirmed by an *ukase* of Catherine II in Dantzig's favour (1767).

This role of guardian, which Russia played toward the rich seaport, was naturally dictated by deeper selfish considerations. The policy of Catherine was as little inclined to give up the purpose of getting possession of Dantzig as had been that of Peter, or Anna, or Elizabeth. There was thus the less disposition in the Cabinet to let the rich spoil of the city go towards enlarging the Prussian share from the partition of Poland. As it was, Frederic was to extend this share far and away beyond what the treaty gave him, by use of unheard-of violence and by deceit in setting the boundaries.

The cautious councillors of Dantzig were wise enough to profit by all these circumstances, in pleading the cause of their safety before the *Czarina* against the Prussian king. The skilled and energetic Willebrandt, who was then Dantzig's agent in St. Petersburg, was able to reach several men of influence: Count Orlow, who had been Catherine's favourite, the influential Saldern, Prince Golizyn, and others. He succeeded in weakening the influence of the Prussian Ambassador on the Neva, Count Solms, and parried his claims to Dantzig. At the same time the Dantzig agent in London, Anderson, invoked his connections in the merchant world of the City, and gave rise to rather more express instructions from Lord Suffolk for Gunning, the English Ambassador in St. Petersburg, in defence of Dantzig. Willebrandt's efforts and the favourable representations of Gunning, were supported also in lively fashion by the friendly and long-acknowledged influence of Holland. Thanks to this, the State Council in St. Petersburg tabled a thoroughly sharp protest against the Prussian designs upon Dantzig. At the end Frederic had to yield.

He did it in his own way. He yielded outwardly, in order the better to spring later on the desired booty, and meantime he took special pay for his concession. Meeting a decided opposition from Russia in the matter of Dantzig, the Prussian King set forth his formal declaration in the Treaty of the First Partition (1772), that "for renouncing all rights to the city of Dantzig and its lands, he takes by way of recompense (*en guise d'équivalent*) the rest of Polish Prussia."

But Frederic the Great did not give up so easily. He never cared for the most sacred treaties, but, just as in the two Silesian and in the Seven Years War, he broke them again with brutal violence. He was the less disposed to bind himself by the first Treaty of Partition, which was in truth nothing else than an act of open international robbery, consecrated by diplomacy. He therefore set about for himself to extend the portion of the spoil his collaborators had assigned to him. The moment he had renounced Dantzig solemnly in the Treaty, he proceeded to demand its seizure. The trouble was that, although the three Powers dividing Poland had signed the contract, a year had to pass before this was sanctioned by the plundered Polish Republic. By that time Frederic thought to better his terms, by forcing the people of Dantzig to renounce Poland and submit to his sceptre.

The refined cynicism with which Frederic set about this compulsory torturing of a defenceless city so long and so cruelly, that it must sometime surrender to his authority, has few parallels in modern history. Injustices have been done, far worse from a material point of view, and bloodier; but there never was a meaner one morally. Frederic began with what the Treaty of Partition had suggested, the immediate taking over of that part of Poland known as Royal or Polish Prussia (West Prussia) and Polish Pomerania, which was assigned to him, and by which he could thus encircle Dantzig.

Free from scruples toward the "territory of Dantzig," guaranteed by the Treaty, he advanced on the spot to its very gates. He forced his way into the suburban communities, and took unquestionably city properties under the sway of Prussia. With his toll turn-pikes he beset the roads from the gates, annoyed the citizens on the way to their suburban villas, and hindered the supply of food from the district. It was a formal blockade of Dantzig. In this way he hoped to crush opposition, and incline the inhabitants to accept his patriarchal lordship.

This was all, however, only the prelude to the most serious blow with which the king meant to surprise and humble the stubborn city. Together with West Prussia and Pomerania he had already taken possession of the twelfth-century monastery of the Cistercians in Oliva, near Dantzig, which contained the tombs of the ancient Pomeranian Princes. In his new role as pious successor of the abbots of Oliva, Frederic now appeared with the gratuitous claim that the whole left bank of the lower Vistula belonged to the monks; and on this principle, with the support of his worthy Minister Hertzberg's learned exposition, he put into effect the liquidation of all this fancied monastic heritage without delay.

Thus in a trice, in the utterest secrecy toward his partners of the Partition, Russia and Austria, the Prussian troops, by the middle of September 1772, had broken into Dantzig's borders, taken Langfuhr and Altschottland, even got control for the time of the peninsula of Hela, and, most important of all, became lords of the port itself. In the Neufahrwasser they hung out the Prussian Eagle, established a Prussian control-station, and began to exact dues from vessels for the benefit of the King's treasury. This meant striking at the very heart of Dantzig.

Joanna Schopenhauer, mother of the famed philosopher, herself a writer of distinction, a member of an old patrician family, writes thus on that day, describing this unheard-of violence, the seizure of the harbour of Dantzig by the troops of Frederic in time of complete peace:

> Like a vampire the Prussian king had fallen upon my unhappy city, committed to destruction, and has sucked out of it its life-blood. This for many a year, until it is fully exhausted.

Under this iron oppression the people of Dantzig soon began to lose their breath. All the time Frederic, without ceasing to strangle them, kept up his system of offering tempting terms as well. The ugly Benoit, his envoy in Warsaw, bought over for him the commission of the Warsaw Diet, set up by the Three Powers to get the partition approved, and incited it against Dantzig. The same Prussian envoy, at the same time, did all in his power to incline the agent of Dantzig in Warsaw, Gralath, against Poland and to surrender his city. In the reports sent by Gralath to the Senate in Dantzig (1773) there is constant mention of Benoit's vehement persuasions "to this frightful step," *i.e.* of cutting off Dantzig from Poland and uniting it with Prussia.

All the time Reichardt, the Prussian Ambassador in Dantzig, was doing his utmost by persuasion and threat, to incline the City Council itself to submission. "My King," he declared cynically, "will have little profit from the trunk, *i.e.* West Prussia, if he does not also get the head," *i.e.* Dantzig. In any case Frederic was resolved to maintain the suzerainty thus secured over the port of Dantzig, as it brought him rich returns, and had some day or other to bring with it the falling of the city itself into his talons.

This last was delayed for the time by the desperate protests of the citizens, their appeal to Holland and England, and chiefly their appeal to Russia. It was the decided opposition of the latter Power that checked Frederic's plan of swallowing up Dantzig for the moment. Yet the thing that helped most of all was the unvarying opposition of the inhabitants themselves. The common people of the parish, especially, manifested the most obstinate stubbornness, even when the Senate began to weaken and yield under obvious pressure. The beggared City Senate and Aldermen were already decided to agree to the fateful submission forced upon them, to accept Frederic's sovereignty over city and port. The affrighted Polish king, poor Stanislaw August, from Warsaw, urged them through the person of Gralath to make this last step.

But the Third Committee would not hear of it. On the other hand, it notified the Merchants' Exchange and the guilds, who gathered at once, and had proclaimed in the public squares that they would rather be buried in the ruins of their city, than have to submit to such sovereignty. The crowd threatened with death any one who dared to act otherwise, and even threw themselves in rage on the Prussian agent and commissioner, whenever these officials showed themselves on the street.

This simple citizen people, partly of Polish extraction, who had drawn a living from Poland for ages, and in whose memory the still ineffaced memory of the murderous Teutonic crimes of old and more recent Prussian brutalities and extortions lived, held to the Republic by unerring instinct, and shrank desperately from the Hohenzollerns.

In view of this attitude of the simple folk of Dantzig and of the Russian objections, Frederic could not realize to the full his plan for Dantzig. His fury knew no bounds. In his first moment of disappointment he thought of new violence. He hit upon the hellish plan of cutting off the city from drinking-water. He ordered the course of the Radunia, from which Dantzig had fresh water, to be deflected, and the water-mains to be cut, in order by this heroic means to bring the city to its knees.

On second thought he shrank, however, from the European scandal which would surely have resulted, and two weeks later withdrew his commands. He finally renounced the idea of Dantzig, so far as he himself, but not so far as Prussia was concerned; and in the Treaty of Partition concluded with the Republic he renewed his promise to renounce solemnly for all time his claims to the city.

Yet he did not cease victimizing the unhappy city to the end of his life, fourteen years later. There was no end of exploiting, of humiliating, of starving it out, with the help of the burdensome Commercial Treaty with Poland. This had been forced upon the latter by the pact of Partition, and excluded Dantzig, as though it were a foreign city, by numberless, savage pretences, taking now one, now another form— cruelties, tariff excesses, police abuses, and abuses in the matter of recruiting. But his chief task, the seizure of the city, Frederic left to his successors. When in his Political Testament he advised them to gather the Republic, as if it were an artichoke or a cabbage, "leaf by leaf, city by city," he had in mind above all the tasty leaf, Dantzig.

Frederic William II, his nephew and successor, remembered the advice. Pretending to knightly nobleness, he was at first welcomed with confidence by the wretched people of Dantzig, who hoped for a respite after the nightmare of his uncle's presence. He was hospitably entertained in the city on passing through, after his uncle's death, to his coronation in Koenigsberg (1786). But the new king was destined rudely to shatter the confidence thus reposed in him. Guided by his first Minister Hertzberg, his uncle's helper in the most shameful attacks upon Dantzig, he went the same way of occupation, although he veiled it by pretended friendship for Poland.

Thus, in his friendly negotiations with the Great Diet of Warsaw, he kept putting forward his wish to have Dantzig as his reward. But the Poles had learned to prize at its true value their jewel, Dantzig, and the city prized more than ever its happy relation to Poland. The consequence was that it disliked more intensely the prospect of being annexed by the hated Prussia, after all the refined martyrdom it had suffered for so many years at the hands of Frederic the Great.

Once more it turned out that the common people of the city, the traders and the working-men, were permeated with the most insistent repugnance to Prussia, and the most loyal temper toward Poland. They had in their veins a large admixture of the ancient, stubborn Kashubian blood and retained the old traditions of bloody encounters with the Order. So the Third Committee sent two delegates of its own accord, two worthy members, Barth and Richter, to the Great Diet, and to King Poniatowski. They brought to Warsaw a solemn appeal, signed by "the most obedient and hard-beset subjects of His Majesty," fifteen speakers for the city, sixty-four members of the Four Quarters, as well as the Elders and Companions of the Third Committee.

Most Serene and Most Gracious Sovereign!—(such was the way in which the defenceless Dantzig turned to the last Polish king, almost in his last hour as sovereign)—The tiny people of Dantzig, whose home on the face of the earth scarcely looks bigger than an ant-hill, has long been unhappy. Panting heavily we await help and relief, and as yet we have not submitted. . . . A piece of bread and Freedom!—that is our cry. Most Serene Lord, our land has been torn in pieces. Our harbour, the rights to which the city has never renounced, is in foreign hands, another is lord over it. . . . We cannot exist longer, unless our territorial possessions that have been taken, together with the port, are returned to us. Most Serene Lord! We stand desperate on a brink, with a madly raging sea of fire round about us. Unless you point us back to the path we were treading until we lost it eighteen years ago (at the First Partition), we must surely fall down into this fiery abyss.

These fears of the citizens were fully justified. It is true that with the death of their worst persecutor, Frederic the Great, they had a somewhat easier life. The export of grain had fallen, thanks to that monarch's crimes, to 9,000 measures in 1782, but it began by degrees to go up again. During the period of the Great Diet it attained an average of some 25,000 measures a year (1789-92), and that when the market prices of rye and wheat were extraordinarily high.

Only the more, however, with these evidences of reviving prosperity did the impatient appetite of the Prussians for Dantzig grow from more to more. The matter of the city became a veritable stone of stumbling in the dealing of Poland with Prussia at the time. Above all it stood in the way of the desired Polish-Prussian alliance. Frederic William II, his sly Minister Hertzberg, and Lucchesini his artful ambassador in Warsaw, made use of every opportunity to get Dantzig from Poland as speedily as possible, without at the same time losing the latter's goodwill. They were even able to throw dust in the eyes of the English Government.

They succeeded in getting the Younger Pitt, then head of the government, to advise Poland to cede Dantzig to Prussia (1790-91). On Pitt's recommendation, Hailes, the honest and friendly but short-sighted English Ambassador in Warsaw, declared himself for this fatal step in repeated public appearances and writings. This all was directly opposed to the ancient friendly relations existing between England

and Poland. It was even opposed to England's own interests, and it can only be explained by the false suggestions made by the Berlin Government, the pretended loyal ally of England and of Poland.

Neither the Warsaw Diet nor Polish public opinion, however, fell a victim to these suggestions. They were guided by a safe and healthy conviction of the national interest in the matter of Dantzig. It is true that, while negotiating with the Berlin Government about a new trade agreement, which would lower the murderous tariffs set up by Frederic the Great, in the trade agreement made fifteen years before, and forced upon the already divided Poland, mention was also made of Dantzig itself. But this was done in order not to provoke Frederic William for the moment, since his support and alliance was absolutely necessary against Catherine. Warsaw had to free itself from the concerted Russian yoke, and carry out needed reforms in administration, in finance, and in the army.

In spite of this, none of the advocates of an alliance with Prussia wanted really to buy it prematurely at the price of Dantzig. Not only did the pro-Russian minority, opposed to the Prussian alliance as such, take its stand fiercely against such a bargain, through the medium of speeches in the Diet, public pamphlets, and proclamations strewn through the streets, but the great patriot Staszyc did the same, though he was on principle in agreement with the majority in the Diet.

He wrote in his celebrated pamphlet, *Warnings for Poland*:

> Let us get us allies. But let us not buy them. Better pay double taxes. . . . Better pay duties at the highest rate, chosen by our traitors from three lower ones. But let us keep an outlet to the sea.

And so it was. The tariff preference and the trade agreement were renounced, but "the sea was kept." Both the Diet and the Cabinet declared most decidedly that Dantzig must irrevocably belong to Poland. The solicitations of Prussia in Berlin and Warsaw were met with polite excuses. Dantzig was assigned at once in 1791 by special mention in the privileges accorded by the Great Diet to the cities, representation in the Diet, and a hearing "which is not to be denied them."

On its own part Dantzig stood with well-proved loyalty behind the Great Diet, and welcomed joyously the famous reforming Constitution of the Third of May. Kahlen, the long-resident agent of the city in Warsaw, did not wish to listen, when Hailes in confidence unwisely tried to win him over to supporting the cession of the city to Prussia. A little later, and from another side, the same man was solicited by Bulhakow, the Russian Minister in Warsaw, in the interests of the pro-Russian Confederation of Targowica, which was already in preparation, aiming to ruin Poland and the Constitution of Third of May. But here, too, Kahlen bore himself worthily, and returned a decided negative.

It happened soon, however, that the Great Diet, and the May Constitution, and the nation, found themselves menaced by the superior might of Russia, by the treachery of Prussia, and by the crime of Targowica, and the peril of a second Partition became visibly nearer. For a moment the idea was entertained of defending the cause of Poland behind the faithful walls of Dantzig. This was in the sorry autumn of 1792, when victorious Targowica took over the administration in Warsaw, under the aegis of Russia; and from the west the might of Prussia was reaching after the chosen booty of Great Poland, as well as for the long-desired keys of Dantzig. At that fateful hour the modest Polish Lieutenant, Stanislaw Fisher, who was partly of German blood, and who later became Kosciuszko's adjutant, and the Chief of Staff for Prince Joseph Poniatowski, first thought of Dantzig. He decided himself to investigate the chances of defending the Republic's only port. He took leave of absence, and went to the seaport city.

Lieutenant Fisher found the Prussians within the city limits, it is true, as they had long made themselves at home in Quadendorf, and even in the Scottish suburb itself. From these points of vantage they thought any fine day to make their way into the very centre of the city. But he found the walls, bastions, and arsenal "in the best of order." What was more, he found the same sentiments among the citizen-body, the merchants, and the guilds, as well as among the body of officers, as had aroused the enduring defenders of Stanislaw fifty years before.

Fisher met the councillors, the youth of the patrician and merchant classes, the officers of the city artillery, the Schuppelius and Niedermayer families, people whose sympathies were with their mother city Dantzig, and who were also warm for Poland. He examined carefully the fortifications and the arsenal. He was amazed at their fine condition, at the considerable stores of weapons and war-gear of every kind. He drank his wine with the youth of the city as a brother. He wept with them in the theatre, whither he was invited to see the noble works of Schiller, redolent of the very spirit of freedom.

These youths of the city, with their names ending in "us," were fired by the best of tempers. They aptly recalled the benefactions and privileges of the Republic, the favour of King Sigmund, the coming of King Stanislaw, and the cannon-balls of Muennich. Above all, they recalled the iron, covetous hand of Frederick the Great, which strangled their trade and prosperity. They shuddered at the sight of the approaching second Partition, and the certainty of their being annexed by Prussia.

On returning to his division, Fisher reported his observations in Dantzig to his friend Vice-Brigadier John Henry Dombrowski, then one of the staff-officers of the Polish Army, and later an illustrious general and patriot. The future creator of the Polish Legions in Italy, a learned expert in military history, knew well the glorious story of the sieges of the city. He formed the purpose of defending it once more, and of using the loyal temper of its inhabitants in an attempt to save Poland from the new peril of division which now threatened her.

Even then, at the beginning of 1793, the Prussians, after crossing the boundary, had occupied Great Poland with strong army corps, and were getting ready to take Dantzig. Dombrowski, in the face of a desperate situation, conceived the bold idea of gathering the Polish army together with the garrison and artillery of Warsaw, of striking at the Prussians, cutting his way through to Dantzig, and there entrenching to await help or some diversion through the French Revolution. Although this extraordinary scheme of Dombrowski did not come into execution, owing to unfavourable circumstances, it was all the same a striking proof of the position enjoyed by Dantzig, both political and military, at the very end of its age-long union with the Republic.

Meanwhile the last hour of Dantzig had struck, both as a Polish and as a free city. In keeping with the treaty for the Second Partition of Poland, made in St. Petersburg, Prussia got the city at last. And she got it in virtue of a most singular and scandalous international pact, as a reward for attacking revolutionary France.

The treaty read:

> The King of Prussia binds himself together with the Roman emperor to take part in the war against the French rebels (*contre les rebelles français*), and not to conclude a separate treaty with them, nor yet a truce. . . . By way of reward for the cost of this war he shall take possession of the lands, cities and districts (of Great Poland), as well as of Dantzig and its territory (*et pour dédommagement des dépenses qu'entraine et entrainera cette guerre*

(contre la France). . . . S. M. Prussienne se mettra en possession de pays, villes et districts de la Grande Pologne) en y ajoutant la ville de Dantzig avec son territoire).

In this unheard-of way, by a robbery of Poland, and as a reward for a robbery of France, Dantzig became the booty of Prussia. A richly-recompensed Russia assented, and an indifferent Europe received the news in silence. On the other hand, it was clear that no hindrance could be offered from the side of the helpless Republic. The Confederation of Targowica, into which Bulhakow had recently wished to draw Dantzig, now handed it over to Prussia in obedience to orders from the Czarina Catherine. The Diet of Grodno, constrained by Russian bayonets, had to confirm the seizure by a new pact of Partition with Prussia.

At the Second Partition, just as at the first, Berlin did not wait at all for the forced assent of Poland, whether from the Diet or from the Confederation. At once it set itself to gather up both the territories of Great Poland and the now at last ripened harvest of Dantzig. The whole scheme for finally consummating this business of annexation was a worthy epilogue to the whole ugly tragedy of violence and villainy which had long tortured the unhappy city. In feverish haste, at the beginning of 1793, Frederic William, in a confidential letter to the Supreme College of War in Berlin, gave orders for the taking of Dantzig by a sudden assault of arms. The lieutenant-general selected for the task, Bruenneck, delayed, however, the execution of this rather risky attack. For his scouting parties reported that the men of the city had foreseen a possible surprise. They doubled their pickets and their vigilance. They had, too, in addition to the regular military garrison, some seven thousand civilian guards for an emergency, as well as eight thousand men "of every estate," ready to defend themselves to the last against the Prussians.

The best that could happen was thus a massacre, only too closely recalling the "surprise" of the Teutons in Dantzig five centuries before. In view of this fact the middle way of political pressure and armed menace was chosen.

A series of most ridiculous demands were set forth, meant to justify the necessity of occupying Dantzig by Prussian armies. The *point de départ* of these fabulous claims—those of the Berlin wolf on the Dantzig lamb which troubled the waters at the mouth of the Vistula— was the imagined Jacobinism of the bloodthirsty people of Dantzig, which threatened the safety of poor Prussia.

That is why the Prussian agent in Dantzig, von Lindenowsky, produced in January 1793 a categorical demand for the handing over of a certain Garnier, a Frenchman said to be a Jacobin envoy of the Paris Convention, who in the previous November had come to the city from Berlin. The City Council, although its investigations did not discover any guilt on Garnier's part, handed him over to the Prussians in fear of charges of provocation. The result was a violent protest, both from the merchants and from the Second and Third Committees, against such a violation of the right of asylum for a French citizen. The upshot was that the Prussian Government made new demands, both because of this "Jacobin" protest, and because of suspected secretion of papers compromising Garnier on the part of the Dantzig authorities.

Meanwhile the end of the month brought the news of the entry into Great Poland of Prussian troops, and of the taking of Thorn. The news was an ominous forecast for Dantzig of its own ruin. It called forth unbounded indignation. Crowds of people walked the streets of the city, hurling threats at the Prussians, urging the inhabitants to arms, and singing the new hymn of liberty, the Marseillaise. At once the Berlin Government began with monstrous charges arising out of these annoying meetings and revolutionary songs. It used the opportunity, too, for making plausible its suspicious deeds in connection with the imminent occupation.

The memorable declaration of Frederic William II, issued in Berlin at the end of February, 1793, in the matter of the city and territory of Dantzig reads:

> The same reasons which moved His Majesty the King of Prussia to send his troops into certain districts of Great Poland, now lay upon him the necessity of seizing the city and territory of Dantzig. Without mentioning here the scarcely amicable attitude of the city for years toward His Majesty, it is certain that it has become of late one of the seats of that vicious sect, the Jacobins, which goes from crime to crime, striving to spread its iniquities on every side with the filthy assistance of its messengers and proselytes. One of these thieves, after trying in vain to spread the poison of his teaching among the happy and deeply loyal Prussian people, was openly received by Dantzig; and even when the facts were explained, it was scarcely possible to get his protectors to give him up.

This fresh example, together with other vices of a falsely understood freedom; furthermore, the secret connexions maintained by French and Polish co-operators in a conspiracy with
that party, which by the boldness of its maxims outweighs the
number of the infinitely more thoughtful citizens; finally, the
ease with which our common foe (the French Republic) can
procure, with the help of friends in Dantzig, every kind of supplies, and especially grain—all these are the symptoms which
have drawn His Majesty's attention to that city. He had thus to
see that it was kept within the limits of action proper to its station, above all in order to secure safety for the Prussian citizens
residing in the neighbourhood.

With this in view. His Majesty the King of Prussia has ordered
the Lieutenant-General de Raumer to take possession of the
city with a sufficient force of troops, in order to keep order
there, and safeguard the general peace. It will be best for the
citizens of Dantzig to serve their cause by prudent and kindly
dependence on the favour of His Majesty by voluntarily admit-
ting His Majesty's armies, and by receiving them as friends.

This capital document is worthy of notice. Apart from the above-
mentioned secret pact of Partition, concluded in St. Petersburg, it is
the one public, official formulation, in the name of the Prussian king
and his government, of the objective, legal and political rights of Prussia to her lordship, or rather, if we take the Prussian official definition,
to her "acquiring" of Dantzig, and her holding it to this day, (at time
of first publication).

"Falsely understood freedom"—this is the dislike of Dantzig for
Prussian bondage; "scarcely amicable attitude"—towards the Prussians
who had victimized the city for thirty years; connexion "with Polish
conspirators"—*i.e.* with its rightful lord and mother-state, personified
in the Great Diet; an inclination for the French Republic—which was
proclaiming the modern watchwords: there you have the villainy of
Dantzig, the imputations under which she was compelled under the
Prussian yoke for over a century.

At the beginning of March General Raumer approached the walls
of Dantzig at the head of a large army, and armed with this royal declaration. He demanded the instant surrender of the chief defences of
the city and the fortress at the mouth of the Vistula, as well as the severance of all trade relations with France. The situation was a desperate

one. There was no prospect of help from any quarter. After three days of noisy deliberation, the view of the merchants prevailed, that the city should be completely surrendered to Prussia, seeing that self-defence was impossible and every support from without was lacking.

But having perforce taken this decision to open the city gates to the armed Prussians, those enemies of Dantzig and of the Republic, the citizens turned with declaration of their due allegiance to the Polish Government in Warsaw. In a dolorous letter "to our King," Stanislaw August, they sorrowfully explained the situation, making it clear that, to save innocent blood and to hinder the complete destruction of the place, "deprived of all counsel and support, cut off from all assistance from Your Royal Majesty," they had found themselves obliged to submit to the overwhelming forces of the enemy. On the other hand, in surrendering by force into Prussian hands, the City Council set express conditions, and won from General Raumer certain fundamental guarantees for the future. These concerned their internal autonomy, their rights to the harbour, to safety of trade and to exemption from military service.

All this amounted to a capitulation on terms, but nevertheless, as was to be foreseen, the Prussians treated it with no kind of respect. In fact, two weeks later, at the end of the month, a categorical "Occupation Paten" arrived from Frankfurt-am-Main, the Grand Headquarters of Frederic William, who, while taking the field against the French Revolution, had heard from Raumer of the readiness of Dantzig to capitulate (*Besitzergreifungspatent*) , This "Patent," with convenient forgetfulness of promises given, rejected all the city's conditions and ordered its immediate seizure. This happened, by a strange coincidence, on the very day of the murder of the Mayor Letczkow and his associates by the Teutonic commander, and just a year before the day of the Warsaw Insurrection, the memorable Thursday of Passion Week, 1793. The Senate, having neither escape nor power, at once ordered the inner fortifications to be given up. Prussian troops were at last to enter the city.

It was then that the last effort at defence on the part of the loyal citizen was made. For a fortnight, since the first agreement with the Prussian general, feeling in the town had been in a state of menacing excitement, and this broke out now in a violent storm. Indignant throngs surrounded the city hall. Amid deafening cheers men demanded war to the last with the Prussian intruder. They thundered at the cowardice and treachery of the Senate. They even began to set the warehouses of wealthy patricians on fire, as traitors to the city and the Republic. Their numbers included, during these demonstrations against the Prussians and for their liberty and Poland, the great majority of the inhabitants: all the petty traders and part of the larger merchants, the guilds, with the butchers at the head, the artisans, and then the labourers, mariners, dockers, and the soldiers belonging to the garrison of the fortress.

This all happened without any encouragement from agonizing Poland, and in fierce defiance of the Prussians. The people's own inborn instinct of self-preservation shrank desperately from dealings with Prussia, and kept firm on the side of Poland. Men rushed to the storming of the arsenal. In a trice they had laid hands on fire-arms. They seized the cannon on the ramparts, and taking by force ammunition from the artillery stores, began to cannonade with grapeshot and rifle-fire the approaching Prussian columns. These, taken by surprise and forced to retreat, opened fire with big guns and from their own lines, so that a large number of the improvised defenders of the city fell as victims.

This time also, just as it happened nearly five centuries before, the "acquisition" of Dantzig by Prussia was accomplished by an act of brutal violence, baptized by and at the cost of the innocent blood of the inhabitants. It was clear that this hopeless effort of the people in defence of their city must be abandoned at once, as the Prussians were in possession of the fortifications. After some days of rioting, there was nothing for it but to submit to the inevitable. At a morning hour of early April the first two regiments of Prussian infantry entered Dantzig through the four open gates of the city. A regiment of dragoons was with them. The citizens looked on in sullen silence. The common crowd broke out in unrestrained curses.

But the soldiers of the city and of the Vistula fortress broke their weapons, declaring that they would not serve the Prussians against Poland and France. The whole garrison, except the officers, were led away as captives, and later on forced to enlist in the Prussian army. A month later, May, 1793, the act of doing homage and swearing fealty to the Prussian King was carried through by his orders. Dignitaries came from Berlin to represent him, and receive the subjection of the city.

Thus did Dantzig come into Prussian hands. Without delay there began a forcible suppression of the ancient republican institutions of the city, which had been so prized hitherto and fostered by Poland.

Then also began an enforced modelling of the city in conformity with the bureaucratic pattern of the other Prussian municipalities. The magistracy was set up on a basis truly and purely official and hierarchical. Faint traces only were left of representation for the merchants and the guilds. Above all, the "Jacobin" Third Committee was of course utterly abolished. The first step of the enlightened Prussian administration went in the direction of obliterating this truly democratic institution, which had remained in Dantzig, the heirloom of the Republic. But the city nobility, composed of the better elements of the merchant and educated classes, felt keenly too the hard fist of Berlin bureaucracy.

Many illustrious men of the city laid down their office in the City Government, the Courts, and the School Board, by way of protest against the Prussian intruder. Some even preferred, not minding the material loss involved, to leave their native city for ever, now that it had fallen under a foreign lord. This, among others, was the course followed by the parents Schopenhauer, as we learn from the memoirs of Joanna, already mentioned, which are full of bitterness at the recollection.

For a time men deceived themselves with the hope of being delivered from the Prussian yoke. But these hopes, originally raised by the triumph of the French Revolution, soon vanished with the conclusion of the Treaty of Basle between France and Prussia.

In spite of this there was formed a few years later an actual conspiracy in Dantzig against the Prussians. This, if not actually organized by the Polish Emigration in Paris and Dombrowski's Legions, was at any rate in close sympathy with them. A handful of students, with the ardent Bartholdy at their head, took up the watchwords of the French Revolution, gathered secretly a few mariners, dockers, and working-men from the harbour, and resolved to raise the standard of armed revolt (1797). Their hope was to restore the former republican liberties of the city.

Even soberer citizens were incited into the conspiracy, men like Father Richter, Deacon of the Church of St. Catherine, known for his irreconcilable attitude to the Prussian Government. The outbreak was fixed for the same Thursday of Passion Week 1797, as it was the anniversary of the recent battle in the streets as well as of the Kosciuszko Insurrection in Warsaw. The conspirators, provided with arms and republican colours, were gathered in the house of Bartholdy. They were to hurl themselves on the Prussian pickets, call the populace to revolt, and get possession of the city and fortress. This childish plot was discovered by the Prussian police. The youthful conspirators were condemned to death in the courts, but the verdict was commuted to a long term of imprisonment.

Under auspices none too promising, auspices such as these, the Prussian administration of Dantzig began. The new monarch, Frederic William II, preferred not to show himself in the city he had fought for so long, in view of the openly hostile temper of the people. When his successor, the young Frederic William III, came to Dantzig in 1798 with his beautiful Queen Louisa, he met with a cool reception from the citizens, in spite of official celebrations and festivals. Nor did he do anything useful, as had always happened when the Polish sovereigns had been welcomed in triumph to Dantzig. He gave no heed to the bitter complaints as to the complete violation of the ancient rights and institutions of the city. With one cheap and questionable benefaction he was content, when he bestowed on certain of the officials of the city, who belonged to the new magistracy, and were most inclined to the Prussian regime, the German nobleman's rank, adding the "von" to their ancient Dantzig names. This titular favour was characteristic of the relations maintained between the authorities in Berlin and Republican Dantzig.

It should be stated, too, that the city did not suffer harm in material respects during the short thirteen years of Prussian rule. Rather did the improvement of Dantzig's trade, which had already manifested itself under the Great Diet, continue under Prussian auspices. Especially did the export of grain during this time advance with strides, so that in 1802 it reached the long since unknown figures of 85,000 measures.

This reacted naturally upon the prosperity of the city. But it was not at all thanks to the Prussian administration, because the latter from the very start made itself felt in the sphere of commerce through its fiscal and bureaucratic tyrannies. It was simply the result of three positive factors. First, Prussia did not at the time possess any ports, except the infinitely worse situated and mal-administered cities of Stettin, Koenigsberg and Memel, which could help in crushing Dantzig by competition. Secondly, in view of the still raging war of the French Revolution and Napoleon with the Coalition in Europe, England, Austria, and Russia, the Kingdom of Prussia, which had withdrawn from the conflict after the Treaty of Basle, was the chiefest, if not the only, source of supply for both parties. Thirdly, and this was the most important fact, after the inclusion of the heart of Poland with Warsaw in Prussia, in virtue of the Second and Third Partitions, the Prussian sources of supply were first and foremost the Polish lands.

If, then, during this period, the last years of the eighteenth and the first of the nineteenth century, the exports of Dantzig, especially of grain, were kept at a high level, it was just for the reason that the city remained, in spite of the Partitions, in intimate touch with Prussian Warsaw; and that in spite of Prussian bondage it remained, as before, a part of the Polish commercial market, which was so profitable to it. Yet, discounting all this, that bondage was a terrible burden both to the whole Prussian part of Poland, to the capital Warsaw, and to the City of Dantzig. Whether here or there, the longing after deliverance was the same.

A Free City

The hour of Dantzig's deliverance struck at last, when Napoleon, after beating the Prussians at Jena, halted his army upon Polish soil. Having come to set Warsaw free from German hands, the emperor turned his special attention at once upon Dantzig; and in January he gave the first orders as to its investment. Marshal Lefebvre, to whom, at the head of the Tenth Corps of the Grand Army, the task was assigned, had the help of the best organized divisions of the Polish army, which was then being formed. This help included the Third Polish Division, that of General Dombrowski, creator of the Legions in Italy; the Polish Northern Legion under Prince Michael Radziwill; and regiments of regular horse, volunteers from the nobility, and the newly formed military units of Posen and Kalish, under Colonel Dziewanowski and Generals Kosinski and Sokolnicki.

The task was an extraordinarily hard one. After the previous year's triumph over Prussia, the present "first Polish campaign" of Napoleon (1806-07) promised to be a heavy one. It was carried on against fresh Russian armies allied to the Prussian remnants, and was marked at the start by the bloody encounter of Eylau, almost a disaster to the French army. Meanwhile Dantzig was well provisioned. The governor, Count Kalckreuth, had a garrison of 17,000 Prussians, 3,000 Russian foot, and three Cossack regiments. He had also access to the sea, from which, as it was wholly in the hands of the Allies, reinforcements kept arriving. Finally there were available the Russian corps of General Kamenskoi, with 6,000 men, and several thousand Prussians under General Buelow. Thus altogether there were over 30,000 troops defending the city.

On the other hand, Napoleon, after the serious losses of Eylau, could not send more than 12,000 men to the Tenth Corps before Dantzig; and there were added later hardly as many more, apart from the divisions lent for a time from the corps of Marshal Lannes and Mortier.

More than once during the siege even the energetic Lefebvre had his moments of despair and doubt as to the issue of the whole matter. Napoleon always roused him, however, in lively and even sharp fashion. The emperor displayed in his whole correspondence with Lefebvre unusual interest in the undertaking, and full knowledge of the minutest details of the situation about the city. At the end of April, 1807, he rode to Marienburg, the ancient Crusader stronghold, which he had taken, as heir of the Polish kings. It appears that he saw Lefebvre in person there, and gave him oral instructions. In any case, as a distinguished Prussian historian of this war, who is now a prominent staff-officer, tells us, direct and telling orders of the emperor in regard to the siege exercised a virtually decisive influence on the capture of the city. More than that, this competent military expert is of opinion that "the importance of Dantzig for the great undertakings" was not appreciated fully either by Frederic William III nor yet by Lefebvre, but only by Napoleon.

The Poles took a major part in the operations, and carried off the honours in the actual capture of Dantzig. They represented a quite presentable fraction of the relatively slender army of investment. They numbered in all some 6,500 men. When Dombrowski, being wounded at Dirschau, laid down his command of the Polish division, it was taken over by the valiant if old and hunch-backed Lieutenant-General Gielgud. These Polish units, hastily gathered, and improvised as they were, left much to be desired in point of organization, and even the most necessary things, such as arms, uniforms, and food, were lacking. Many had only light military overcoats, and beneath them any sort of clothing. The poor fellows suffered cruelly from cold, rain, often from hunger, being in the trenches before the city during the worst season of the year.

The siege of the city proper, apart from preliminaries in February, began in March, and the cannonade in earnest in April, 1807. One must remember that the position of the French army after Eylau was far from favourable and its temper rather depressed.

In spite of all this, the Poles, speedily ridding themselves of occasional distempers at the start, not only did their duty at Dantzig, "holding the very centre of the line of assault," on the "most dangerous and most important station," but even by their endurance, firmness, and impetus they came to be the pick of Lefebvre's army. The marshal soon knew their value, and loved them. In his daily orders he did them justice repeatedly, giving honourable mention to their officers and privates. Once indeed, when an enemy's sally from the city was being repulsed, he dismounted from his horse, unbuttoned his coat in order to show his marshal's embroidery and stars, and at the head of Downarowicz's Polish battalion, himself led a splendid counter-attack, snatching the drum from the drummer's own hands.

The consciousness that they were fighting for a Polish Dantzig and a Polish sea-front served above all to maintain the high level of courage among the Polish troops. More than one fine expression of this feeling was given. The anniversary of the Constitution of the Third of May was solemnly celebrated in the lines. In a fiery speech delivered on this occasion by Father Przybylski, chaplain of the First Infantry Regiment, Prince Sulkowski's, the men were reminded of "the waving banner of Poland on the shores of the Baltic." Time and again in the appeals and reports of Dombrowski, Gielgud, and their subordinates around Dantzig, this notion of their efforts and fights being a way of emancipation is most clearly emphasized.

But from the other side, and in Dantzig itself, the great majority of the citizens saw for the first time in the siege of their city an act of justice and emancipation. Convinced of this in their souls, these loyal patriots for the first time took almost no part in the defence. The Prussian Royal Family, fleeing from Berlin after the disaster at Jena, thought for a time of seeking shelter behind the city's walls; but in view of the cool attitude of the inhabitants they thought it better after a short stay to flee still farther to Koenigsberg and Memel. They obviously realized that it was not possible at least for Hohenzollerns to expect such affection and shelter from the people of the city as Stanislaw Leszczynski once enjoyed.

The effort made later by Count Krockow to form in Dantzig a corps of volunteers for Prussia met with complete failure. The Count himself for that matter soon fell into the hands of the besieging Polish troops. Equally unsuccessful were the appeals of the Governor Kalckreuth for loyal generosity on the city's part towards Prussia. On the other hand, the real temper of the inhabitants is revealed by the fact that he had to take special measures of precaution for the Thursday of Passion Week, 1807, through fear of riots on that memorable anti-Teutonic and anti-Prussian anniversary.

Worse still, the citizens maintained secret communications with the Polish outposts, furnishing necessary information and assisting the privates of the garrison to desert. This was so common that, according to Gielgud's figures, "over 4,000 Prussian deserters, Poles and Germans, passed through the Polish line, of whom 700 Poles enlisted voluntarily in our regiments."

Colonel Krukowiecki, who was in command of the first rank of Polish outposts, wrote:

> As far as the citizens of Dantzig are concerned they are all of good cheer, and await impatiently the moment when the beneficent hand of our saviour (Napoleon) will set them free from the Prussians and Muscovites.

The last serious effort to relieve Dantzig from the sea side was made at the beginning of May, with the landing of considerable Russian and Prussian reinforcements at the mouth of the Vistula. The valiant and successful repulse of this peril by the Polish troops represents their finest and most meritorious performance during the whole siege. It made the speedy surrender of the city inevitable. The fight was of the bloodiest and fiercest, as the Poles and French gave no quarter, and victory had to be bought by heavy losses. Here in this battle the young and gallant Colonel Anthony Parys fell, shot through the breast by a rifle bullet as he was leading his regiment to a final charge. He was a splendid officer of the Polish Legions in Italy, and the true hero of the present struggle for Dantzig.

On the spot where he fell his companions threw up a mound and held a solemn funeral in his honour. The illustrious writer and patriot Prince Alexander Sapieha, who was a member of Gielgud's staff, exclaimed at the funeral, in the presence of the city, which still held out:

> Heroic Race of Poles!
>
> The weakness of our fathers has not availed to erase the glory of their ancestors. Turn your gaze from this hill whither a holy ceremony has led us. Look upon Dantzig, for whose restoration to the motherland you are fighting. Fix your eyes in this direction to the endless plains of Pomerania, torn from us by treachery. For centuries we cherished this land in safety. . . . Ye see this moving element, the stretches of the Baltic which the eye cannot measure. That was our possession during the time of the Sigmunds. Polish vessels ploughed its surface, and brought abundance into our land by flourishing trade.
>
> All this glory our ancestors handed over to their children, and

it is now your task to recover what the carelessness of the latter let slip. . . . We have piled up this mound with our hands. . . . Perhaps some day, when fortune ceases to harass us, Poles will recover their former possessions, and surrounded by their children will point to this grave as an evidence of our deeds, and as a lesson of how much it cost to bring a fallen nation to a new birth.

The names of Parys and of many other Poles who took part in these battles, and received in return the generous mark of the French Legion of Honour, were mentioned with high distinction in the bulletins of the Grand Army at the end of the siege and capture of Dantzig. In fact, at the end of May, a few days after the unsuccessful attempt at relief, the capitulation followed. Scarcely a month passed from the proper commencement of the siege before all was over. It is a notable fact that of all the investments of Dantzig the shortest was this one, in which the city was taken from the Prussians.

Marshal Lefebvre, by way of doing homage to the Poles, assigned them the place of honour when the city was occupied, both because of their proved valour and because they had the real right to the city. At the solemn entry into the city through the High Gate on the morning of May 27, 1807, the marshal, surrounded by his suite, led the way in a blaze of decorations, and right behind, in full parade, with a band playing at its head, the Polish Legion followed. The six regiments of French infantry brought up the rear.

The capture of Dantzig was an event of the first rank, not only military but also political. It finely restored the position of the Grand Army, and made possible the decisive victory at Friedland a few weeks later. Napoleon, aware beyond all others of the significance of the event, expressed his personal satisfaction to Lefebvre in a beautiful letter, granting him the dignity of "Duke of Dantzig."

In those very days of triumph the emperor made his entry into Dantzig. Welcomed cordially by the inhabitants, as were the Polish kings of yore, he took up his residence in Langgarten. He inspected with care the chief institutions of the city, the fortress of the Vistula, the Neufahrwasser harbour. He received in special audience representatives of the council and the merchant-class. He took from their hands a memorial, which set forth the sore crimes suffered at the hands of the Prussian Government from the time of the First Partition. He showed special satisfaction towards the Polish besieging forces. A review was held on the Long Square. He covered them with proofs of his favour and appreciation.

As a matter of fact Dantzig was won largely at the price of Polish blood. The aged General Gielgud emphasizes this in his report made to the emperor:

> The Third Polish Division, which I had the honour to command, came to the blockade of Dantzig with 6,500 men under arms. As a result of the labours of the siege and the losses sustained in skirmishes and in the trenches, it numbers now but 4,650 men.

The Polish losses were thus some two thousand. He went on:

> The inhabitants of the city are Poles. They are imbued with the spirit of loyalty and admiration for Your Imperial and Royal Majesty, as well as with feelings of love for their former motherland, when Poland was still a united nation.

At that time neither the future of the city was certain, nor yet the issue of the war itself. Nevertheless it was generally taken for granted that, with the triumph of Napoleon and the reconstitution of Poland, Dantzig should be returned to her motherland. Such was too the general opinion of Warsaw. It was to be expected that the first news of the taking of Dantzig by the Franco-Polish army should give rise to universal enthusiasm in the capital.

> The news was the occasion of such great rejoicing in Warsaw that on the very day it came all the houses in the city were illumined, though no such order had been given by the authorities. . . . On all the streets were to be heard the glad cheers: "Long live the great Napoleon, the deliverer of Dantzig!

At once the President of the Warsaw Provisional Regency Commission, the grey-haired Malachowski, who had been Marshal of the Great Diet, prepared a letter to the Emperor asking for the assignation, or rather the restoration, "of the city of Dantzig and all the parts of Poland round about her"—i.e. Royal Prussia and Polish Pomerania—to the Polish State in the hour of its rebirth.

Nevertheless, things were to turn out quite differently. When a little later, after the victory of Friedland, the Peace of Tilsit was concluded between Napoleon and Czar Alexander, the latter's rooted opposition served above all to make the reconstitution of a large and powerful

Poland impossible. The result was the mangled Duchy of Warsaw as a compromise, without Royal Prussia and Pomerania, and without Dantzig. By the Treaty of Tilsit of July, 1807, Dantzig, with the territory round about to a radius of sixteen kilometres, was declared a free and independent city. At the same time the free use of the Vistula was guaranteed. In December, thanks to the kind mediation of the French Marshal Soult, the boundaries were somewhat extended by a supplementary agreement made in Elbing between Dantzig and Prussia.

Though left nominally under the joint care of Prussia and Saxony-Warsaw, Dantzig actually was at the immediate disposition of Napoleon himself, whose bust in marble took the place in the Town Hall formerly occupied by that of Frederic William. The city was given a French garrison and a French commander, General Rapp. A considerable war contribution, with numerous supplementary payments, was levied in the interests of the French Treasury. In return the town got back its constitution and the machinery of self-government: the Three Committees, the Council called officially from now on the Senate, its own courts, representations of the four "quarters," etc. At the emperor's command, however, the Code Napoléon was introduced. The citizens managed to get this greatly delayed and make it only an auxiliary institution.

Besides the governor, the resident French agent, Massias, held office, and afterwards also the Saxon-Warsaw one, Helbig. There were in addition quartered here, rather for purposes of espionage, the Prussian Consul Vegesack and the Russian Trefurt. The people of Dantzig had their official deputation now in Paris, as formerly in Warsaw, together with a permanent envoy with power to act, Kahlen, who had been the representative to the Republic of Poland in Warsaw of old, and was now the same for Napoleon. It is worthy of note that recommendations kept being made by the emperor to the Dantzig delegates, just as formerly by the Kings Sigmund and Sobieski, to the effect that the city should admit Catholics to its offices and its administration.

From the autumn of 1808 the garrison in Dantzig was composed of two Polish regiments of foot of the Duchy of Warsaw. The commander was General Grabowski, who in the next year succeeded Rapp as Governor, the latter being placed on the emperor's staff for the Austrian campaign of 1809. After Grabowski, the duties of commander were performed for a time by General Woyczynski. The relations of the citizens with the Polish garrison and the Polish commanders were always of the best. In 1810 Prince Joseph Poniatowski, War Minister and Commander-in-Chief of the army of the Duchy of Warsaw, came to Dantzig to inspect the garrison and the fortress. He was received by the city with great honours, as nephew of the late King Stanislaw August and the most popular of Poles, and with the respect always shown to the royal Polish line.

In accordance with Napoleon's own orders and in agreement with the military authorities in Warsaw, headlong efforts were being made all this time to strengthen the fortifications of the city. In the spring of 1811, after the first misunderstandings between the *Czar* and Napoleon, Dantzig was placed under a state of siege, as it was especially threatened from Russian quarters. On the outbreak of the great war with Russia, Napoleon, on his way to Moscow, visited Dantzig for the second time in June, 1812, in order with his own eyes to verify the state of its defences. It was to be one of the chief bases for all further operations against Moscow. This time also he received in a long audience representatives of the city authorities and the merchants. With the penetration and simplicity peculiar to him, be questioned them in detail as to their needs and burdens, as well as about the actual industrial position of their free city, which he had called back to life and retained under his protection.

The position of Dantzig during this protectorate left, it is true, very much to be desired. The six years of Napoleon's rule had brought it to the verge of ruin. Its trade had wholly ceased. Many of the oldest and richest of its financial houses had become beggared, bankruptcies were numerous, the artisans had no work, and the working-classes were in misery. The people kept themselves alive with grants from the army or work at the fortifications. It suffices to note that the population of the city with the surrounding district was diminished by one-fourth. It had been over 80,000, and was now only 64,000.

The causes of this disastrous situation were many. The contributions and numerous military levies of the French were a sore burden to the city. The blockade of the continent was infinitely more harmful. Instituted six months before the capture of Dantzig, by the famous Berlin Decree (1806), which declared the British Isles to be in a state of blockade, it cut the city off from its chief customers and providers overseas. Both imports and exports were as good as finished for Dantzig. Neither the emperor's "licences" granted to the citizens, nor exceptional vessels and ladings, could help the matter, nor yet the spread of contraband. Chiefest of all, the Tilsit solution itself of the question of Dantzig and Poland, forced upon Napoleon by Alexander, was absolutely mistaken, absurd, both hurtful for Poland and ruinous for Dantzig.

The so-called "free city," cut off by West Prussia from Poland, found itself in virtually the same position, and without escape, as after the First Partition. Rather the position was even worse than after the Third Partition, when Dantzig had at least been reunited with Warsaw, beneath the Prussian yoke it is true, but at least under one single regime. To return to her natural and historical state unity with a free Poland, as one of the most splendid of Polish cities, a city animated with a fullness of life, and not to vegetate as a fancied free city in an artificial separation and isolation from her—this has been and will be the highest political injunction imposed on Dantzig both by nature and by history. Indeed, the most striking proofs of this are furnished by the lamentable experiences of the free city during the Napoleonic era.

Meanwhile the tragic end of this epoch was approaching. The disastrous retreat from Moscow followed. Rapp, who had been taken again by the emperor on that luckless expedition, returned to Dantzig in December, 1812, half alive, with face and hands frozen, but full of energy. He at once declared that the city was in a state of war.

Already the Russian Army was following close on the heels of the retiring remnants of the Grand Army. True, no one in Alexander's army headquarters had settled the matter at this juncture (New Year, 1813) how far the victorious pursuit was to be pushed. In the most approved circles of Russian politics, and just because Napoleon was in such desperate straits, it was not thought in the least desirable for Alexander to pursue his foe to France itself. Such an expedition would have had the appearance of advantage for Russia, but would have meant in reality the reconstitution of Prussia.

Kutuzow, the Russian commander-in-chief, was decidedly of opinion that a stop should be made at the Vistula, that an alliance with Prussia was undesirable, as was also further fighting *pour le roi de Prusse.* He wanted, on the other hand, to come to terms with Napoleon and make peace on the best conditions for Russia. The Chancellor Rumianzeff was of the same opinion, as was also almost the whole suite and the "general public sentiment" of Russia. In the same way a modern Russian historian and military expert, after weighing the whole military and political situation of that time, came to the conclusion that precisely this and no other solution suited "the real interests" of Russia.

Thus, then, these best possible conditions of peace, of which Kutuzow was thinking, and which were not hard to obtain from Napoleon in view of his position, involved not only the uniting of the whole Duchy of Warsaw to Russia, but also the gaining of the line of the Vistula from end to end. This meant at once the incorporation of the whole of East Prussia. The situation seemed once more the same as it was in the time of Czarina Elizabeth, when striking at Frederic the Great. As a matter of fact, just as in the former time, this whole province of Prussia was actually now in Russian hands.

According to a competent eyewitness, Field-Marshal Boyen, a Prussian who conferred with Czar Alexander at the end of 1812, the Russian military party demanded unconditionally the Vistula as a boundary-line.

They were ready at this price to leave the rest of Europe to Napoleon, or to even the devil himself.

The whole latter part of the Moscow campaign, the escape of Napoleon, the slowing-up in his pursuit, is all virtually explained by the above secret calculation of Russia. In point of fact it looked seriously as if the calculation were to be realized. In January, 1813, the Russian generals, Tchernisheff and Rydygier took Koenigsberg. Here a highly curious regime was begun, without the least regard for Frederic William III, and beneath the most serene authority of the Czar Alexander himself, just as of yore under Czarina Elizabeth. The Russian military governor, Marquis Paulucci, had taken Memel even earlier, abolished the Prussian administration, taken over the treasury, and simply instituted a Russian government.

The question of Dantzig was closely connected with these important events. There can be no doubt that the Russian plans at the end of 1812 and during the greater part of 1813 had one aim in view—to get possession of Dantzig and either simply retain it or, in the worst case, leave it with the status of a free city as the Peace of Tilsit had done. There would, of course, be one difference—that the protector would be Alexander and not Napoleon.

In fact, Kutuzow, in a very remarkable ordinance addressed to General Wittgenstein, advised him to remove the Prussian troops from Dantzig and use for its investment only Russian units. The result was that in January, 1813, after the city was surrounded, the Cossack Commander Platow was in charge, whilst in February Wittgenstein, and to the end of April General Lewis, directed the operations. In

May Prince Alexander of Würtemberg, Military Governor of White Russia, the born uncle of the *Czar* himself, was sent straight from the Russian headquarters. The choice of such a distinguished personage, as well as the increase of the besieging army to well over 30,000 men, were a clear indication of the importance attached in the immediate entourage of the *Czar* to his getting control of Dantzig himself.

Frederic William, too, easily scented the danger, and gave orders already in April "to make all thinkable efforts" to send to the siege of Dantzig Prussian divisions, whose very presence would be a kind of pledge of Prussia's claims to the city. A weak division of Prussian *"Landwehr,"* numbering a few thousand men, under the leadership of Count Dohna, was brought together, and it was sent in June "to the help "of Prince Würtemberg.

The Russian commander naturally received the uninvited "help" in the most ungracious manner. He looked down on them, issued orders to them in Russian, just as to his "crews of reserves," but set them regularly in the rear, etc. Thus there was played out under the walls of Dantzig a strange tragedy-comedy, part political, part military, between the Prussian troops, who outdid themselves in their importunate eagerness, and the Russian Commander, who turned the cold shoulder mercilessly to their proffered services.

This last siege of Dantzig, in the year 1813, when, as in 1734, it was beset and finally taken by victorious Russian armies, was once again nothing less than a tragedy alike for Dantzig and France and Poland. Again Polish and French troops defended the city in her bitter need. It was infinitely important for Napoleon that Dantzig should hold out as long as possible—"that walled palladium of France on faraway reaches"—as it would be for him a solid *point d'appui* in case of a more fortunate turn of events.

Yet the garrison gathered now in the city, the Tenth Corps of the Grand Army, was nought but a collection of frozen, wounded, and exhausted wrecks of men, survivors of the fearful catastrophe of Moscow. It was a "heap of invalids," numbering nominally over 35,000 men, of whom, however, the greater part—up to 18,000—at once went into hospital, and soon died almost to the last man. There were thus in truth never more than some 13,000 to 14,000 men fit to bear arms. It was the most complete medley of people—French, Bavarians, Dutch, Westphalians, Spaniards, Italians, and even Africans.

Next to the French, the stoutest element of defence which was to be found in the garrison, was the Poles. The Seventh Polish Division was there, under the command of Brigadier-General Prince Michael Radziwill. There were three regiments of foot, the Fifth, the Ninth, and the Eleventh, which had taken a brilliant part in the capture of Dantzig six years before, and were now called upon to defend it. There was the Ninth Regiment of Polish Lancers, which had just shed its blood liberally and distinguished itself in the Moscow expedition. Finally, there were two companies of foot and one of horse artillery, and a company of sappers. This made a total of 6,000 men, virtually half of the whole garrison that was able to fight. All were splendid soldiers, resolved to defend the ancient Polish city to the last.

Of course the Russian besiegers on their part undertook vigorous steps the moment the city was invested, to demoralize and win over precisely this stoutest Polish element of the garrison. The Russian commander himself prepared a proclamation urging the Poles to desertion and treachery. At the same time a falsified appeal was issued, supposed to be that "of the citizens of Warsaw to their brethren in the field." In this proclamation the people of Warsaw adjured and challenged all Poles under arms in general, and those defending Dantzig in particular, "by the sacredness of their faith and of their fatherland," to leave the standard of the atheistic and crime-committing Napoleon and to place themselves at once under the protection of "the great *Czar*, Alexander the Magnificent," and of "the great Russian nation," akin to the Poles in blood, in language, and in near neighbourhood.

This singular appeal, written for the rest in curiously bad Polish and full of Russianisms, was naturally a wretched counterfeit. As a matter of fact, Warsaw, when captured at the beginning of February, 1813, by the Russian armies, maintained generally a patriotic and hostile attitude to its conquerors. Instead of urging people to desert, she did exactly the opposite. Her whole soul was with the Polish Army fighting in the field under Prince Poniatowski and holding loyally to France and to Napoleon. All the same, the moment the Russian armies approached Dantzig, Cossack officers sent by Platow put in an appearance among the Polish outposts and began to fraternize. When they were hustled out they ride away, scattering among the troops a host of the proclamations above mentioned.

The Governor, Rapp, was equal to the occasion, acting like a soldier and to the point. He wrote up the whole incident in the *Dantzig Gazette*, ordered the counterfeit appeal "from Warsaw" to be printed word for word, and bade it be read everywhere publicly to the assembled Polish regiments. The result was that the troops rejected with indignation the Russian request, and took a solemn oath to hold out unfailingly in the defence of Dantzig, France and Napoleon.

They issued further a written declaration, edited by Captain Wladislaw Ostrowski, who was then at the head of the Polish Horse Artillery at Dantzig. He defended the city gallantly, and became in 1831 the zealous marshal of the famed Revolutionary Diet in Warsaw. The declaration recalled the Partitions of Poland, the massacre of Praga, the injuries without number suffered from the Powers who had divided the land, especially from Russia, and ended with a pledge "of love of country and gratitude to Napoleon."

This declaration, which was handed to Rapp by Prince Radziwill and the Polish Staff, was signed by:

> The generals and senior officers, the commanders, the officers and non-commissioned, as well as the privates of the Fifth, Tenth, and Eleventh Regiments of Foot, the Ninth Regiment of Lancers, the commander, officers, non-commissioned and privates of the Foot and Horse Artillery and of the Sappers (in Dantzig).

This eloquent pledge was confirmed by the Poles time after time by their splendid deeds. During the first attack made in earnest by Lewis on the city early in March, 1813, the Russian columns advancing to storm the place were scattered, thanks chiefly to the furious charge of the Polish Brigade. The grateful Rapp appeared from that time in the red cap of a Polish Confederate and often in full Polish uniform.

The conditions of the still continuing siege grew day by day more desperate. Beneath the enemy's fire, under the influence of hunger, typhus, and insidious tales from without, the spirits of the men kept sinking always the more. When treachery was creeping into the city and among the Allies, only the Poles remained true to their duty, to their leader, their nation, and to Europe, loyal to the end here, just as on the field of Leipsic under Poniatowski. Nearly half of them— some 2,500—died, either falling on the ramparts or dying in the city hospitals.

At length, a month after the Battle of Leipsic, when he had exhausted his means of defence and there was now no more hope, Rapp signed a deed of surrender on honourable terms at the end of November, 1813. He was to leave the city with his garrison on New Year's Day, 1814, if no relief came before that time.

By the deed of surrender the Poles of the garrison were guaranteed the choice either of marching out and making their way to Napoleon's armies or of returning home. Alexander, however, for reasons which did him no credit, refused to ratify the terms. He ordered the French, together with their commander, to be taken prisoners and sent off into the depths of Russia. The Poles were allowed to return to Warsaw, but without their arms.

At ten o'clock in the morning of New Year's Day, 1814, some 3,000 Polish troops, with 230 officers, marched out of Dantzig by the Oliva Gate, under the command of Radziwill. They had their arms with them, but laid them down a league outside the walls. This was the last Polish garrison to take leave of the Polish Dantzig for over a century.

The Prussians, who were keeping a suspicious eye on the Prince of Würtemberg, were deeply alarmed at the news of the surrender of the city, a transaction arranged by the French governor with the Russian commander, of course without any thought for Berlin. At once they informed their king that the Russian staff was resolved to level the fortifications of Dantzig, not to restore it to the Prussian crown, but to declare it a free city. At the same time they denounced:

> Certain gentlemen of the Senate of Dantzig, who certainly desire a return of the city's former glory and exert an influence on some important persons here. (*i.e.* in the Russian headquarters.)

Frederic William sent an order forthwith naming General Massenbach as governor and Colonel Dohna as commander of the city.

Now, however, as the Prussian historian of the fortress of Dantzig expresses it, a "catastrophe" followed. The Prince of Würtemberg declared outright that he had no intention of obeying the king's orders, that he awaited the orders of the *Czar*, and that duty bade him consider above everything else the interests of his master and Russia. For the rest he added quite openly that in his opinion "the question of Dantzig is inseparably bound up with that of Poland."

The Russians, then, the day after the Franco-Polish garrison left the place, entered Dantzig themselves. The keys were sent to the *Czar*. Lieutenant-General Prince Wolkonski became governor of the city and General Rachmanow the commander. The Prussians were excluded wholly both from the military and the civilian administration. Permission was given them to man just the inner Heugarten Gate, between the Bishop's Hill and the Hagelsberg.

Sharp differences soon resulted. A violent scene took place between the prince and the Prussian generals. Count Dohna was bold enough to post up printed proclamations in the city on his own authority as "Commander." But these were torn down at once, and that possibly by the people themselves, who, as the confidential reports of Major Hake to the Prussian king inform us, demonstrated in a clear manner their hatred of the Prussian authorities. The Prince of Würtemberg threatened Dohna himself with arrest. For a month the Russians were sole lords of Dantzig, and made themselves at home in the city. Thus, at least for the short period of January, 1814, the old Russian longings of Peter and Elizabeth for the city were fulfilled.

Nevertheless the Prussians did not neglect their business. From the moment when, renouncing Napoleon, they joined the Coalition again, they undertook with great diligence the regaining of Dantzig. In February of 1813, on the first negotiations of Frederic William with the *Czar* as his ally, the Prussian demanded that Russia bind herself to restore Dantzig to him. Alexander demurred at the time, and in the joint agreement of Breslau-Kalish between Prussia and Russia, he made no mention of the city at all. Nor did he cease demurring in the matter, for one or another reason, during the whole spring and autumn campaign of 1813. Even in October, after the Battle of Leipzig, he broached the idea through one of his diplomats of leaving Dantzig as a free city, or in any case not letting Prussia get it back.

But both the Prussian diplomats and the king himself kept assailing the *Czar* in this delicate matter with ever-increasing insistence. Unfortunately, too, they got the support of the British representative in the Allied camp, Lord Castlereagh, the Secretary of State for Foreign Affairs, who took a most perverted view of the Dantzig question, as indeed of that of Poland as a whole. Castlereagh, by the suggestions of the Prussian Cabinet, was daily kept in dread of the Russian peril, and recalling the mistaken and now out-of-date initiative of Pitt of twenty years previously, he declared himself favourable to the restoration of Dantzig to Prussia.

In the face of this Alexander could not resist further. When, then, on his victorious way to France, he received in Basle the news of the surrender of the city to the Prince of Würtemberg, he gave orders that it be restored again to Prussia. These orders reached Dantzig at the beginning of February, 1814, and were carried out forthwith. Thus the Prussians got possession of Dantzig once more, and that for a full century.

Nevertheless, in spite of the *Czar's* orders and the act of Prussia in again taking over the city, the fundamental question of its title to Dantzig remained still an unsettled one. It was a matter for the whole of Europe, which, just like all the others growing out of the division of the lands taken from Napoleon, and of his abdication and the capture of Paris, had to be settled finally by the General Congress of the Nations in Vienna. It was on this that the unhappy people of Dantzig set their last feeble expectations. For these experienced and stubborn citizens, just as in the days of Frederic William III, or with Frederic the Great, shuddered at the thought of coming again under the rule of Prussia.

They did not at all admit themselves beaten. They did everything they could to prevent their again falling into Prussian hands. As indicated, the resident representative in Paris, "deputy of the city of Dantzig at the Emperor's Court," in Napoleon's time was first the patron of Dantzig Kahlen, and after his death in 1811, his friend Dr. Keidel, a resourceful and energetic man, born in Bremen. The Senate of Dantzig, through its closed Committee of five senators, foreseeing the fall of Napoleon and an upheaval in Europe, worked out secret instructions for Keidel immediately after the disastrous retreat from Moscow.

These instructions, under the date of January, 1813, set forth on the eve of a reconstitution of Europe the essential demands of Dantzig. The return of the city under the Prussian sceptre was entirely excluded, as the greatest of evils, a thing quite inadmissible. But in the same way the Constitution of the city of 1807 as a free city was declared to be unsuccessful and undesirable for the future. For this situation led, so the report declared, to similar lamentable results for the city as had been experienced from 1772 to 1793, while it was cut off from Poland. Those grievous experiences proved that Dantzig could not maintain itself as a free city, even though all its sovereign rights were guaranteed. Thus, then, the instructions ended, the best solution, and the one we must aim at, would be that Dantzig be again united "with Poland, as a powerful and independent State."

After waiting through the critical year 1813 and the siege of the city, Keidel began with the desired representations to the Allied Powers the moment their victorious armies entered Paris. He first reached the *Czar* through the latter's Swiss friend Laharpe, and handed him in May, in the name of the Senate of Dantzig, a bold and dexterous memorial on the question of the unlucky city. He recalled the oppression and violence it had suffered at the hands of Frederic the Great and his successor. He declared the seizure of the city by Prussia in virtue of the Second Partition to be an act which international law did not warrant. He went back to the plans of the Czarinas Anne and Catherine as guardians of the city. He demonstrated that:

> Dantzig is the key to the Vistula, and the natural and indispensable market-place of the products and output of Poland.

> Therefore, these very Polish lands are most concerned for the maintenance of an independent Dantzig.

Keidel demanded, therefore, from Alexander the deliverance of Dantzig from Prussia, and the reservation for her in the future at least of the same guarantees of a free city as had been given at Tilsit, this time, of course, under the protectorate of the *Czar*. Properly speaking, he departed here from his secret instructions, whose chief recommendation was the uniting of the city with Poland.

But this very reconstitution of Poland was still, during the stay of the Allies in Paris, a very doubtful thing. Then, again, the Allied statesman, Pozzo di Borgo the Russian diplomat and a convinced enemy of the Poles, Metternich and Stadion the Austrian statesmen, to whom the Dantzig representative turned for counsel, did not in the least favour the restoration of Poland by Alexander. In any case Keidel, in all his papers laid before the Allies at the time in Paris, unconditionally excluded Dantzig's return to the Prussian domination. At the same time he went privately to the British Embassy in Paris and put into the hands of the ambassador, Sir Charles Stuart, a separate and still more cogent memorial, which was meant for Castlereagh. In this he recalled the former friendly relations of Dantzig with England. He stated emphatically that:

> His Majesty the King of Great Britain never ratified the delivering up of Dantzig to the Prussian king, done temporarily in 1793 and then abolished in 1807.

Dantzig's representative in Paris, in his search for salvation for his city, received, as was natural, the support of a most distinguished Pole who was present in the city. Prince Adam Czartoryski. This nobleman, who was then the friend and confidant of the *Czar*, took Keidel under his protection, and with him the cause of Dantzig he was championing.

Czartoryski wrote about Keidel in his Paris Diary of the time:

The man works very well. He is an excellent man; he is stirring up compassion in commercial cities for his own.

The prince himself for a year and a half had worked with the greatest industry at the reconstitution of Poland by way of a personal union with Russia, even if it had to be under the sceptre of the *Czar*, since better conditions could not be realised.

In the light of this idea of a new-born Poland for which Czartoryski was working, against Kutuzow's plan of complete conquest, the cause of Dantzig assumed a fresh complexion, and turned into its normal historical path. The goal now was no more the taking over of Dantzig by the *Czar* in the spirit of the greed for extension shown by Peter and Elizabeth, but the rightful restoration in one form or another of the ancient and proper relation of the city to Alexander as King of Poland. This would have meant, of course, the greatest political and industrial gain both for the future Kingdom of Poland and for Dantzig itself. And it would be in exact agreement with the essential recommendations of the secret instructions prepared by the Senate.

With this idea, prompted by Czartoryski and armed with his recommendations, Keidel crossed to London, in order, as the representative of the Dantzig Senate, to continue there his efforts for saving his city from Prussia. He found in the city time-worn sympathies for Dantzig, and used them. Two distinguished members of the Union of London Merchants, Isaac Solly and Lewis Paleske, instituted a plan of intervention in the Dantzig interests. In the same way Keidel got in touch with the Opposition in Parliament and the Press. In his difficult task in London there helped him an eminent Pole who was staying in England, Count Joseph Sierakowski, a friend of Kosciuszko, whom Czartoryski had recommended to him.

In August and September, 1814, the Opposition *Morning Chronicle* printed several articles inspired by Keidel which concluded decidedly against the delivering up of Dantzig into Prussian hands. One of these was written by Sierakowski. The view of the paper was that the occupying of Dantzig by Prussia after the surrender of Rapp and the withdrawal of the Russians was to be considered as only a temporary expedient. Void of all legal justification, it should be rendered void by the decision of the nations of Europe in favour of a return to the former independence of a free city.

But all of Keidel's movements were being watched with the greatest care by the Prussian Embassy in London, and reported to the Chancellor Hardenberg in Berlin. They were also being represented to the British Government, which was at the time under Prussian influence, as highly suspicious actions and hostile to the cause of the Allies. It was thus in vain that the tireless representative of Dantzig knocked at the doors of that Government. He turned, it is true, in person to the Prime Minister, Lord Liverpool, and to the head of the Foreign Department, Lord Castlereagh. He presented again a huge memorial, in which he went back to the privileges granted by Casimir Jagiellon. He demanded the deliverance of his city from Prussian hands, and the guarantee for free traffic on the Vistula. He claimed finally—and this in the spirit of the suggestions of Prince Czartoryski—that Dantzig should be put "under the cover of the special protection" (*sous l'égide d'une protection spéci*ale) of the future King of Poland. Unfortunately the eloquent representations of the Dantzig deputy did not convince the British statesmen, whose fear of Russia made them the more well-disposed to Prussia.

It was with difficulty that Keidel, as Sierakowski told the prince, obtained from the British Government permission to attend the Vienna Congress. Apart from that he gained nothing; "rather Lord Liverpool talked to him profusely about the kindliness of the Prussian Government." To crown the whole, Weickhmann, a member of the secret Committee of the Dantzig Senate of the former year, who was now named mayor of the city by the Prussian Government, sent to Hardenberg in Berlin the whole secret declaration, together with Keidel's confidential correspondence. The Prussians could thus, with their exact acquaintance with the facts, take successful steps to checkmate all that was being done for the city.

Keidel did indeed get to the Vienna Congress, 1814-15, but all his efforts in Dantzig's cause were easily paralysed by Hardenberg. Nor did the mediation of Czartoryski avail any more. He held his ground longer, it is true, in the matter of the defence of Thorn and its incorporation into the Kingdom of Poland. But even this point was resigned; and in the face of the unfriendly attitude of the Powers, the efforts made to save Dantzig were the less able to command success. By the treaties of Vienna, made in May and June, 1815, between the Powers that had divided Poland, as well as by the Act of the Conclusion of the Congress, Dantzig was finally assigned to Prussia.

It turned out in very truth that the final disposal of Dantzig by the nations was achieved under extraordinary circumstances. For it was done in the teeth of the city's own wish; and her remarkable protests before the whole of Europe, her efforts to the very last to avoid being relegated again to the domination of Prussia, seemed worthy of more detailed mention.

At the same time the decision of the Congress of Vienna, which assigned Dantzig to Prussia, was taken not the least because of the then prevailing anxieties about a Russian hegemony in Europe, if the latter were to swallow up East Prussia. Circumstances had now changed wholly. Such fears had vanished. Mighty Russia has fallen at the hands of Prussian Germany, which has also been striving after the hegemony. In view of the restoration of an independent Polish Republic, the verdict of Vienna must be thoroughly revised in the matter of Dantzig, and that in the light of its age-long, natural, and historical connexion with Poland.

In the Hands of Prussia and Germany

With the recovery of Dantzig by the Prussians there began in the city a work of centralisation and of Germanization. In February 1814 a special Organizing Commission, sent from Berlin, dissolved the previous municipal administration of the free city, which was suspected of Franco-Polish sympathies. It set up instead a new City Council, composed of creatures of the Prussian Government. It further transformed on the same principle the character of the city courts, dismissed the Code Napoléon, and restored the Prussian *Landrecht*. It abolished every trace of the Polish and French institutions of the free city, and adapted everywhere the general Prussian municipal administration in their place.

On the new division of West Prussia into the departments of Dantzig and Marienburg, Dantzig was made the capital of the whole province in 1816, and became, under that most capable, clever, and convinced Germanizing bureaucrat, Oberpraesident Theodore Schoen, the seat of a provincial bureaucracy, whose numbers were legion. This able administrator, and still abler destroyer of all things Polish, was at once a Liberal and an ultra-Prussian, and is one of the spiritual fathers of the later National-Liberal idea and of Hakatism. With the help of an assistant, who was worthy of him, Flottwell, who was at the time Regency Councillor in the city and became later the famous Oberpraesident of Posen, he accomplished in the eight years of his stay in Dantzig an extraordinarily successful piece of work for German *kultur*. He did much for the improvement of the administration, the rebuilding of the city, the roads, streets, and schools, everything with the studied, easily-running purpose of Prussianizing.

His work of *oberpraesident* was begun with distinction. He undertook the restoration of the old Castle of the Grand Master in Marien-burg, which has been destroyed by the people of Dantzig and the Poles together, as a visible symbol of the renewal of the Crusaders' supremacy (1817). Simultaneously he secured financial support and administrative privileges from the government for the active assistance of the business world of Dantzig, which had suffered, and was threat-ened with complete ruin after the recent industrial and military sub-versions.

By these methods and by his own personal influence Schoen made the first really successful breach in the bitter anti-Prussian front the people of Dantzig had maintained, because of their traditional inclina-tion to Poland, and pushed forward markedly the work of transform-ing the ancient Polish city into a Prussian emporium.

All the same, these skilful operations of a superfine bureaucracy could neither hide nor repair the actual disaster the change brought upon the city, thus severing it from the natural source of its well-being, its nursing Alma Mater, from Poland. As yet, of course, the industrial misfortune consequent on this severance was not felt so keenly dur-ing the first period of Prussian occupation, after the Second and Third Partitions, since at that time a considerable part of Poland, including Warsaw, had shared Dantzig's fate of remaining under Prussia. But in the epoch which began after the Congress of Vienna, and lasted a whole century, the position of the city was at least so far changed for the worse that Poland's one port was finally cut off from the new Pol-ish State set up by the Congress.

The results were very soon apparent. The trade of Dantzig lost the normal guarantees of its prosperity and improvement. For the time being the Berlin Government was able by a dexterous method of using its influence in St. Petersburg, and by dint of clever nego-tiation in trade matters with Russia, by the palliative of a profitable Customs-treaty to stimulate it artificially. But in spite of all this, it was condemned to a gradual and inevitable end. Misery made its appear-ance in the formerly wealthy city among the patrician merchants and among the common people, who had been producers, or who had lived on the traffic in timber, on the warehouses, or on the harbour itself. And this was no more merely transitional, as during the war in Napoleon's time. It clearly pointed to the unavoidable, if gradual, im-poverishment and decay of the city.

The population became aware of their crumbling fortunes, and their resentment became general. It was not long before violent riots occurred in the city, caused by the general poverty—a thing unheard of before in Dantzig. They happened in September 1819, August 1821, and May 1822.

LEONAUR

ALSO FROM LEONAUR
AVAILABLE IN SOFTCOVER OR HARDCOVER WITH DUST JACKET

THE FALL OF THE MOGHUL EMPIRE OF HINDUSTAN *by H. G. Keene*—By the beginning of the nineteenth century, as British and Indian armies under Lake and Wellesley dominated the scene, a little over half a century of conflict brought the Moghul Empire to its knees.

LADY SALE'S AFGHANISTAN *by Florentia Sale*—An Indomitable Victorian Lady's Account of the Retreat from Kabul During the First Afghan War.

THE CAMPAIGN OF MAGENTA AND SOLFERINO 1859 *by Harold Carmichael Wylly*—The Decisive Conflict for the Unification of Italy.

FRENCH'S CAVALRY CAMPAIGN *by J. G. Maydon*—A Special Correspondent's View of British Army Mounted Troops During the Boer War.

CAVALRY AT WATERLOO *by Sir Evelyn Wood*—British Mounted Troops During the Campaign of 1815.

THE SUBALTERN *by George Robert Gleig*—The Experiences of an Officer of the 85th Light Infantry During the Peninsular War.

NAPOLEON AT BAY, 1814 *by F. Loraine Petre*—The Campaigns to the Fall of the First Empire.

NAPOLEON AND THE CAMPAIGN OF 1806 *by Colonel Vachée*—The Napoleonic Method of Organisation and Command to the Battles of Jena & Auerstädt.

THE COMPLETE ADVENTURES IN THE CONNAUGHT RANGERS *by William Grattan*—The 88th Regiment during the Napoleonic Wars by a Serving Officer.

BUGLER AND OFFICER OF THE RIFLES *by William Green & Harry Smith*—With the 95th (Rifles) during the Peninsular & Waterloo Campaigns of the Napoleonic Wars.

NAPOLEONIC WAR STORIES *by Sir Arthur Quiller-Couch*—Tales of soldiers, spies, battles & sieges from the Peninsular & Waterloo campaigns.

CAPTAIN OF THE 95TH (RIFLES) *by Jonathan Leach*—An officer of Wellington's sharpshooters during the Peninsular, South of France and Waterloo campaigns of the Napoleonic wars.

RIFLEMAN COSTELLO *by Edward Costello*—The adventures of a soldier of the 95th (Rifles) in the Peninsular & Waterloo Campaigns of the Napoleonic wars.

www.ingramcontent.com/pod-product-compliance
Lightning Source LLC
Chambersburg PA
CBHW031902090426
42741CB00005B/603